The Awakening

A Journey of Self-Discovery
and Personal Vibration

By
Rocky Troiani
The author of My Tormented Mind

MAPLE
PUBLISHERS

The Awakening: A Journey of Self-Discovery and Personal Vibration

Author: Rocky Troiani

Copyright © Rocky Troiani (2023)

The right of Rocky Troiani to be identified as author of this work has been asserted by the author in accordance with section 77 and 78 of the Copyright, Designs and Patents Act 1988.

First published in 2023.

ISBN 978-1-915996-59-6 (Paperback)
      978-1-915996-60-2 (Hardback)
      978-1-915996-61-9 (E-Book)

Book Cover Design and Layout by:
    White Magic Studios
    www.whitemagicstudios.co.uk

Published by:
    Maple Publishers
    Fairbourne Drive, Atterbury,
    Milton Keynes,
    MK10 9RG, UK
    www.maplepublishers.com

A CIP catalogue record for this title is available from the British Library.

Contents

Chapter 1 – The Awakening.. 14

Chapter 2 – Focus and Motivation 21

Chapter 3 – Nikola Tesla – 'The Genius' 31

Chapter 4 – Spiritual Meditation.................................... 39

Chapter 5 – The Meaning of Life..................................... 49

Chapter 6 – The Law of Vibration: The Primary Law........................... 58

Chapter 7 – The Sun of God 68

Chapter 8 – Awakening of Nature 75

Chapter 9 – Healing and Well-Being.............................. 84

Chapter 10 – The Universe is Talking to You................. 92

Chapter 11 – Pure Unconditional Love.........................103

Chapter 12 – Self-Discovery and Personal Vibration 113

Chapter 13 – Epilogue...120

Chapter 14 – To the Reader 126

Dedication

With infinite gratitude, I wish to dedicate this book to my guide, Julie Lucas, for empowering me to rejoice in the returning light of my spirit.

"Just when the caterpillar thought the world was over,
it became a butterfly."

– *CHUANG TZU*

Acknowledgements

First, and always, I wish to acknowledge the source of everything in this book and everything that is life.

Second, I wish to thank the beautiful people whom I call my saints. My counsellor and now friend, Julie Lucas, opened a door to my soul – which had been closed for decades – to let in the light. She helped me walk through my childhood into peace. A new world was born.

Third, it is clear to me who my true friends are – those who have stood beside me through thick and thin. They know who they are: a handful of souls who held me up in my darkest days. Friends I call my family. Friends who, in addition to my parents, have been there for me – and who saved my life. Sadly, my parents are no longer with me. I lost my father at the age of twenty-two, and my beautiful mother died from internal bleeding due to a dispensary error by our local pharmacy.

My first book, *My Tormented Mind*, which I wrote after losing her, gives a detailed account of my journey – a journey of negative energy from the age of seven, when I was subjected to sexual and mental abuse, which led to drug abuse, prison and, in my later years, alcohol abuse. It was a journey I never wished for, one which almost cost me my life.

I acknowledge, with pure devotion, my mother and father. My final promise is to make them proud of me and to show them I am capable of making something of my life, despite the journey I was placed on at a young age. I believe that journey happened for a reason, just as I believe everything in life happens for a reason.

I wish to acknowledge little princess Lyrah, my angel who walks beside me. I kiss her photo every day to tell her I love her, as I do photos of my mother and father. Their energies live on in me in this life and will do into the next.

I also want to say a warm thank you to Vrinda and John of White Magic Studios for their kind support in publishing both my first book and now my second. I wish to take a moment to thank Shirley 'B', my silent angel. I truly love you.

This book is phase two of my journey. I don't claim to be a skilled author, but I write from my soul, in my own words, in my own way. As I approach my fifty-third year, I realise what life is all about – what our purpose is on earth. *The Awakening* will show you my discovery, my awakening. I hope you can interpret my story, to deliver your own discovery.

I have been blessed with a glorious moment: a moment of vision and clarity. I could not have done this without my beautiful friends. I thank those who have accepted me but refused to accept the parts of my journey I didn't choose.

I wish to give a heartfelt thank you to a truly inspirational man: former SBS special forces soldier and member of the hit TV series *SAS: Who Dares Wins* and founder of Break-Point Ollie Ollerton. Ollie attended my book launch for *My Tormented Mind* and his amazing support marks true friendship.

Last but not least, the great energy, the creator of all, that higher power in the universe and its frequencies – I sincerely thank you.

Foreword

"You can't change anything in your external world, until you change the energy of who you are."

The true secret of happiness and success is locked within us all. We just have to know where to look, and then the answers will be revealed. Many souls lose their way on this journey called life, and few manage to regain control through a deep understanding of the principle of energy and how that relates to humanity. Rocky Troiani is one of those few!

After our meeting in 2022, it was clear to me that Rocky had found the secret to change. In *The Awakening*, Rocky shares that journey for one single intention: to educate and help as many people as possible to live a happier, healthier, more fulfilling life.

This is a roller coaster of a story – compelling at every stage – a must-read for all who see the light or those engaged in growth. I am honoured to call Rocky a friend and a fellow author.

Ollie Ollerton

SAS Australia

Channel 4 *SAS: Who Dares Wins*

Founder of The BreakPoint Academy

Introduction

The story you are about to read is a true account of my journey. This journey almost cost me my life.

I suffered a serious amount of trauma during my childhood – trauma that wasn't recognised until years later when I lost my mother in tragic circumstances. Unrecognised trauma can lead to a traumatic lifestyle and deliver serious mental health issues.

On 13 January 2021, I attempted to take my own life. Life had beaten the life out of me. I didn't recognise myself any more and I didn't know who I was or where I was going. When you hit rock bottom, the depths of darkness and the ice-cold breath of death on your face are all too real.

Life is a journey, not a destination. At every step, you will be faced with choices that will determine the person you are. If you constantly have the big picture in mind and take time to make the right decisions rather than the easiest way out, you'll be able to look back on your journey and be proud.

Some people are blessed with a beautiful journey; some battle their way through mental health problems, relationship problems, family issues, and, in some cases, want to end their life. In 2022, I was introduced to Julie Lucas, a professional counsellor. I had already been introduced to the NHS mental health team, which I found exceptionally clinical: two chairs and a table in a room with no pictures, nothing. This form of counselling was not for me – I was suffering severe mental health issues. Losing my mother had opened up many emotional scars. My past trauma had finally come to a head. The mental health team's answer was to give me heaps of medication, which only covered up those scars and disabled me from getting to the root of my problems.

Meeting Julie saved my life. As the weeks and months went on, I was introduced to myself as a child through meditation. I met myself, the seven-year-old boy who had suffered mental abuse from a family member and was made to feel inadequate, small and insignificant. I could see myself sat in a cold room, isolated, afraid of life, afraid of people. Julie asked me to hold the boy's hand. As I did, I was told to walk their image into the light. From that very moment on, my life changed dramatically. My soul was released from the darkness after almost fifty years of loneliness. From being a weak, tired, drained child, I was taken into the light.

For many months after losing my mother, I would attend a beautifully tranquil place called the Aylesford Priory. Among a row of twenty or so memorial benches was a bench with no plaque. The week after my first counselling session, I returned to the Aylesford Priory. After five months of visiting, the bench now had a plaque, which reads: 'Shirley B, a loving, devoted mother, who is sadly missed and truly loved. A true angel of life.' Was this a coincidence or was this a message from a higher power? It was as if the planets, the universe, the earth, its entirety – God, as you can call it – had moved everything into place.

I started listening to motivational videos on YouTube. I came across a remarkable scientist called Nikola Tesla, whose inventions include the Tesla coil, alternating current (AC) electricity, and the discovery of the rotary magnetic field. Nikola Tesla in my opinion stands head and shoulders above all other researchers and inventors. His discoveries of the secrets of the universe in terms of energy and frequency and vibrations are truly amazing. I couldn't let go of this: it had opened my soul, which had then opened my eyes to another dimension.

I'd never known who I was and what my purpose was. My very negative upbringing had led to a very negative adult life. If the vibrational frequency of the people around you is negative, that energy will transfer onto you. I realised I needed to change my direction. Every business venture I had attempted had failed. Every relationship I had entered had failed. Even my own family had failed me. Why? Was this all by chance again? Or was my life meant to resemble the memorial bench, finally finding its identity? From my counselling with Julie to opening my eyes to a guiding spiritual energy, I now have an identity.

I would love this book to help open your spiritual energy. I want to help you discover your purpose in life and for you to surround yourself with positive people. I can only express my own discovery, but finding vibrational frequency has been truly uplifting for me. For however many years I have left on this beautiful earth, I will use my vibrational frequency to live a positive and happy life.

Throughout this book, I explain how I discovered the power of personal vibration. If just one person out of a hundred discovers this through my experiences, then the God of energy has blessed me with a purpose. If I can be encouraged by the God of energy to grant myself forgiveness for my failings and not live in fear and guilt but to always keep trying to live a more positive version of myself, then I believe you can be encouraged too.

Understanding Frequency

Life is a process of self-discovery, and no experience is ever wasted. It only brings us closer to our evolution. It was not until I was lost that I began to discover both myself and my purpose. I was now entering the greatest adventure of my life. During my suffering, I found my truest self. *The Awakening* is the discovery of my journey and understanding the true meaning of vibrational frequency.

I will start by briefly describing what frequency and vibrations are. Every single human being has a field of energy. Our bodies are made up of particles that are in constant motion, which vibrate and create energy. In short, this is your vibrational field. We live in what many people call an ocean of motion, where everything is built of small molecules that are constantly vibrating. One easy way to determine if you're vibrating at a high frequency is by concentrating on how you feel physically. If you feel upbeat and full of energy, that indicates you're vibrating on a high frequency. If you're feeling low, extremely tired and generally not happy, that indicates you're operating on a low frequency.

Here's a simple example of vibrational frequency. Let's imagine you have two tuning forks. If you tap one of the forks and then place it close to the other, you'll hear a vibrational sound, which will transmit to the other tuning fork. These vibrations generate electromagnetic energy waves. These waves can even dictate how your body is functioning.

Another example: you've probably at one time or another walked in somewhere and felt a bad vibe about the place. This would suggest your vibrational frequency is not tuning into the atmosphere around you.

I have another example: picture two droplets of water that are slowly moving towards each other. When they get close enough, they will attract each other and become one droplet instead of two. This is because they are like vibration. A droplet of oil and a droplet of water, however, would not become one because their vibrations are different.

Everything that surrounds us is filled with energy. Vibrational energy manifests an unseen force that drives all physical matter to convulse in different frequencies. Vibrational energy can be thought of as a state of being, the environment, or the energetic quality of people, atmospheres, places, thoughts or acts.

You can actually alter your vibration by changing the way you think, feel and act. Within your mind is a field of energy, and the millions of thoughts you have every day create motions which simultaneously send out vibrational waves. This is where the law of attraction comes in. The law of attraction means 'like attracts like'. Whatever frequency you are vibrating at attracts a similar vibration.

When you meet someone, you can immediately understand a little bit about their personality, just by the energy their vibration gives off. I continuously had negative people around me. After losing my father in 1992, my life took a tumble. My vibe was bad, which meant I received that bad vibe back. This led the way for a very traumatic journey. In my experience, what you give out, you receive in return. Only now, in my fifties, have I discovered this.

We might ask ourselves why we are not gifted with this discovery in our younger years – after all, it would make for a truly beautiful life. My answer to that is simple: wisdom is the greatest teacher. Without it, we gain no knowledge and without knowledge, no lessons are learnt.

When you finally experience the alignment, everything becomes comforting and your life and soul become as one. I pay close attention to my surroundings. Always be aware of how you feel at a specific moment in time.

Even for myself, writing this book has been an education. Through further research, I have discovered other beautiful avenues to experiment with, and I hope to write more books to bring enlightenment to people's frequencies. I wish to live my remaining years content in the thought that when I finally close my eyes on this life, I'll have given it my all, my best shot. I wasted decades being a person I never understood, but now, following counselling, I aim to live a life of fulfilment. Counselling opened a closed door and, with it, pure peace.

I hope you will enjoy and understand the importance of finding your happy place in life too.

Chapter 1

The Awakening

In the summer of 2022, during my counselling sessions with Julie, an extraordinary phenomenon occurred: a higher power began communicating with me. Let me explain.

I was in a truly dark place. The counselling was opening new doors and closing old doors within my soul. My personal life was destroyed, my professional life was in pieces and, emotionally, I'd been beaten to my knees. I began writing my emotions down on paper and found it an amazing therapy for my mind. Counselling and writing gave me clarity about what I was feeling and lifted a huge weight from my shoulders. I cannot express how therapeutic it is writing about your life. It released the trauma from my soul and cleansed my mind. It was as if I was writing to a higher power and letting go of the hatred within me. My childhood trauma, a little girl I'd been fundraising for passing away, then my mother dying had all taken a toll on my mental health.

To my surprise, as I scribbled out the last of the bitter answerable questions of my life and prepared to toss my pen aside, my hand remained poised, as if by some invisible force. An idea had entered my mind: I was going to publish the story of my life. Coming up with the title of my book was very easy: it was to be called *My Tormented Mind*.

It took me approximately four months to complete. During this time I emailed White Magic Studios, which deals with book publishing. I just loved their name. It seemed to fit perfectly, in some strange way. An amazing gentleman named John telephoned me. John was extremely enthusiastic about publishing my book and so I sent him my manuscript. I signed an agreement with the publishers – they loved my story. The book of my life was due to be published. This was a huge achievement for me, it really was. I poured my heart out to help others understand a little more about the purpose of life.

Life was moving in a very strange way for me. An unseen discovery. A new journey with a new chapter ahead. I was approaching a turning point. My close family were now gone, and those who were left had no interest in my well-being in any way, shape or form. It was time to move on and close the door on my past. Something unexplainable was happening within me, something spiritual. I was communicating with deep thought. I like to use mental images because, as a communication tool, thoughts are often more effective than words. But I also used the vehicle of experience – the experience of life – to communicate. When feelings, thoughts and experience failed me, I would use words.

Sometimes I would sit on Shirley B's memorial bench at Aylesford Priory and talk to her, because I could feel her beside me. Rather than talk to Shirley in my head, I would speak to her aloud. It was as if I was having a conversation with a spiritual force. I am a strong believer that if something gives you comfort, regardless of what people think, don't be shy of that process and use it to your advantage. In my case, words were my release and talking worked for me. My counselling taught me to express my feelings with words. If I let my mind do the talking, I didn't feel the same release.

I started talking to myself a lot, much more than normal. I would have arguments with myself; I would tell myself off; I would praise myself if I felt happy. This process of talking was something very spiritual. It was helping me, and I felt as if something was listening to me. A lot of people would think this was the first sign of madness; however, this was far from madness. I began to listen to my heart rather than my mind. I began to discover that the heart is an energy; it being a spiritual energy was the only way I could explain this. I started using my experience as my messenger and I discovered that if I didn't listen to it, I would keep reliving the past and ignore the purpose of my life. All in all, I was being guided by an invisible energy force.

Julie taught me how to meditate, which has proved incredibly beneficial for my mind. I would sit on Shirley B's bench to meditate and pray and listen to my energy. I found great energy from an old tree in the grounds. I did a little research and found out it's well over a hundred years old. Every time I visited, I would place my hand on this beautiful tree and draw energy from it. Why did I feel energised after touching this tree? Why did I feel energised by Shirley's memorial bench? What was lifting me? I began to question religion, my perception of faith, how I saw God. This was a remarkable awakening. I was beginning to understand something very clear: that by tuning my energy into the earth, nature and the universe, this invisible force was beginning to teach me its values.

The energy I was gaining from this whole experience was teaching me something very powerful: the force of connecting with the earth. I started taking note of the nature around me. For over a year and a half, I regularly visited Aylesford Priory. During the summer of 2022, when I prayed, I prayed to the sun. I felt as if it was listening to me, to my soul. Every time I left Aylesford Priory, I felt energised. Every time I left my counselling sessions with Julie, I felt energised.

I continued to attend my mother's and my father's graves every day, and have done so for over a year and a half. My mother was a very devoted Italian Catholic and an incredibly spiritual lady. I had a religious upbringing, which comforted me. Knowing something might be listening to me – a higher power, God, Jesus, something spiritual, an energy – brought me peace.

It was through watching motivational videos that I came across a fascinating man called Nikola Tesla. His understanding of the connection with the universe, the earth, the sun, the stars, the moon, its entirety, its energy was something I was beginning to learn to understand.

When I was sixteen, I had an out-of-body experience (bearing in mind I had no understanding of what an out-of-body experience was at the time). I remember going to bed and placing my head on the pillow, then rising from my bed and floating to the corner of the room. I remember looking at my arms and seeing nothing but bright-red electricity. I then looked at myself asleep in bed and, at that point, drifted back to my body. I ran downstairs to my mother and father and told them what had just happened. I think they thought I'd been dreaming, but I knew for sure it wasn't a dream. That experience has stayed with me and I now understand what it was.

✱✱✱

I don't believe things just happen by chance. They happen for a reason, and we can tune into that reason and learn to understand its energy. Everything that was happening to me then, I was going to embrace and work with.

One day, I felt the need to visit a memorial in Gillingham, in the Great Lines Heritage Park. Something was drawing me to this memorial. My father, Ronald Sands, and his father and generations before him, served in the Royal Navy. My father served forty-seven years at Chatham Dockyard. When I was seven years old, I said to him that I wished to join the Navy. He said no, it wouldn't be for me. For many years, I dreamt of being at sea: I'd be on ships and battleships, and sometimes they'd be stranded in the mud. I still dream of the sea now. On this particular visit, I wanted to seek out the name of Sands. I found three names: Mr C Sands, Mr H Sands and Mr T Sands. Prior to changing my name in 2007 to Rocky Troiani, my name was Clive Sands. I felt an immediate connection with Mr C Sands. For some time now, I've meditated at this memorial and prayed to all those wonderful men and women who lost their lives for our freedom.

What was happening to me – why all this discovery? It was as if a jigsaw was being pieced together, and the final parts were now in place. I began to learn that everything is a frequency we can't see, but a frequency far more powerful than anything we could ever imagine.

✱✱✱

For some years now I have been running my own charitable organisation, Bring Every Kind Smile (BEKS). BEKS is named after a very beautiful friend of mine, Rebecca Watts, who lost her life to cancer. Since 2016, I have been supporting families with sick and terminally ill children, making wishes come true and creating memorable days for those who will be left behind once the child has passed.

I began to question why I felt the need to give hope and smiles to people suffering, when I had spent many years suffering myself. I started answering my questions. The moon, the stars, the sun, the universe – they were all putting things into place for my forthcoming journey. The energy surrounding me was so powerful. On a daily basis, I would say, "I'm going to be OK." I didn't just say that in my head, but out loud. I still do it now because it gives me emotional support and encouragement. I am confident; I am strong; I am getting better every day. Affirmations give clarity and strength to my energy. They lift my vibrational frequency to another level.

The very cold, dark place I had been in for years was becoming a place of the past. A new energy had been born. I got back to weight training and fitness training and began to follow Ollie Ollerton on YouTube. Ollie is a former SBS special forces soldier and was part of the Channel 4 TV series *SAS: Who Dares Wins*. He's the founder of Break-Point, which delivers 'performance tools and insights developed from Special Forces expertise'. Ollie has also published *Break Point*, his amazing true story. This guy really intrigued me. I listened to his stories about how he approached dealing with trauma and I connected with what he said. One podcast episode that stands out for me is his one with the Mulligan Brothers. Sometimes, there are people who inspire you in such a powerful way – Ollie is one of those people.

Everything in my life was now looking stronger. I felt I had suffered enough, and if I didn't let go of my demons, if I didn't let go of my past, it would end up killing me. I discovered for myself that God is an energy, a powerful energy that connects with every star in the universe, with the sun, the moon and the earth. Everything has a vibration. I wanted to learn about the secrets of the universe and its energy, frequency and vibration. I don't believe we are physical beings in a physical universe, but vibrational beings in a vibrational universe. We are transmitters and receivers of energy. Living as a vibrational being is something I am still learning and embracing day by day.

I lived a very negative life, surrounding myself with very negative people of very low frequencies, including members of my own family. As a vibrational being, you will either attract or fend off vibrational frequencies, events and experiences. We naturally attract what we are in harmony with and repel what we are out of sync with. If you're walking down the street and you say good morning and smile, you'll encourage people to smile with you. But if you look at somebody in a negative way, they will look at you in a negative way too. Whatever signals you put out, you get back.

You could work hard on all your goals, dreams and ambitions, strive for every inch of success, but if your frequency isn't in tune with the universe, those goals and ambitions won't ever arrive. No matter how hard you try, things won't fall into place. But by changing our vibrational frequency and aligning ourselves with the universe, we can manifest the things we want and they'll come to us without too much effort. If you're afraid or anxious, you'll attract afraid and anxious people. Everything that happens in the inner world reflects what happens in the outer world. The outer world is just an echo of the inner world.

Act as if your goals have been there all along, as though your inner world and your outer world are aligned. So many people drag their way through life, unhappy in the same job for decades, never realising their true potential. Never be vague with your desires. Be positive, think positive, act positive and you'll become positive. The universe will generate what you want. Use visualisation to raise your vibrations. It's one of the most powerful tools for finding your happy place. When you visualise what you want, your mind is unable to differentiate between what's real and what's not. When your heart, mind and soul are in tune with one another, you can visualise your desires, taste them, smell them, feel them.

Look at me: I've written a book – someone who can't read or write properly, failed everything at school and was even expelled. I proved to myself I could write a book and have it published. Anything is possible. When you have faith in yourself and you work in line with the universe, it delivers energy, strength and positivity. I will continue to write further books, as I become more experienced, to show my friends, and the public, that there is something out there beyond what can be explained.

I want this book to be my bible, my faith, my understanding of life, my angel, my guide, my world, my universe. In it, I am going to explain how to work in line with the universe and how I used my positive research to guide me to a better place. If one person reads this and finds hope and stability, then I've done my job well. Of course, this throws open the question as to what choice is highest. And that philosophical question has been asked since the beginning of time. If the question engages you, you are already on your way to mastery.

We are unique beings. Express your inner self, prove to yourself you can achieve anything you want. At fifty-two years of age, I have found my spiritual ground. I have found my feet – and they are firmly planted in connection with the earth, the universe, the moon and the stars. I don't want to live in the past any more. It bred negativity for over fifty years. I have made the choice and I have found something so beautiful that I wish to share with you.

"Self-realisation is the truth of consciousness."

– ROCKY TROIANI

Chapter 2

Focus and Motivation

There will be an abundance of opportunities which will leave you discouraged, make you lose your passion, make you think it's not meant to be. If you give up at the first hurdle – or the second – or the third, what that really means is you never wanted it bad enough.

You have to find something you truly believe in – an objective for success – and be relentless in achieving your goal. You can't ever tell yourself you'll never know what it looks like, what it feels like and what it tastes like. Don't fear how long it may take. Don't give up because people don't have faith in you and tell you it's not possible. What your attitude needs to be is, I won't stop believing, I have faith in myself and I will find the frequency to tune myself into positive, successful people.

You need to learn to not take no for an answer and not settle for mediocrity. You will strive to keep pursuing what's in your heart. Sometimes your mind will play tricks on you: it will convince you it's not possible, that little niggling voice at the back of your mind, no matter how hard you tell yourself you'll succeed. Say out loud: I will succeed, I will find my purpose in life, I will have what I'm wishing for and I will become far more ambitious than I've ever been.

Ask yourself what you really want from life. Get a pen and paper and write it down so you can see it. After writing *My Tormented Mind*, I assessed my life in great detail. Writing things down is a fantastic way to work out all those unanswered questions. Your mind creates visions: sometimes they're bad; sometimes they're good; and sometimes they let you down by throwing you into confusion. I really recommend noting down your ambition. You have to want it bad enough to visualise it in detail. Keeping that competitive edge alive will maintain a positive level of vibrational frequency, which will attract others to you.

Take time to mentally prepare. The body has limitations; the heart, your spirit vibrational frequency, does not. We focus so much on what goes on from the neck down, we forget where it all really starts from – the power of the mind. If you haven't changed your mind to think positively, then teach yourself to set your frequency to a positive place or you won't be physically prepared either. And that's where the preparation starts. What would your life be like if you looked towards the future and decided you're not going to allow your fears to stop you from achieving your ambition. Whatever you want to do, do it. If you want to change jobs, do it. Otherwise, you'll be stuck in the same, mundane job you hate getting up for every morning – you'll regret putting your shoes on to do something you absolutely detest every single day. You do have a choice.

When life beats you to your knees, for whatever reason – depression, anxiety, lack of trust, lack of faith in yourself – what happens is, you end up surrendering. Some people turn to crime, drink or drugs for an easy way out. Trust me, people, that is not the answer. Don't let your negative thoughts eat you up. We have to fail in order to learn, because from every failure we are taught a lesson. You have to be tough on yourself. Success is always under construction. There is never a clear visible path to take; you just need to condition your thoughts. Successful people have a relentless attitude for success. They don't give up at any hurdle. They believe in their journey, despite what other people may think.

Sometimes we take so many knocks we struggle to get back on our feet. Believe me when I say you have to get back up – you don't have a choice. If you sit and dwell on whatever's holding you back, you won't succeed. The negative world you've become accustomed to will hold you there until you work on bettering yourself and cultivating a stronger mindset to boost your productivity.

You have to have challenges in life. And the only way to overcome challenges is to start walking forward, without looking back. Take that step, every day. No matter what you are facing, get up and start walking. You need to visualise the end result – act like you already have your goal. It's an amazing way of convincing your mind. Others will pick up on your frequency.

If things were so easy to obtain, we'd all be wealthy and be where we want to be. When I was little, I was made to feel insignificant. I was convinced I was a worthless human being. The same family member poisoned my mind for decades. I was programmed to fail – and fail I certainly did. Until now. I want to help you reprogramme your mind for success on all levels.

Most people dread accepting responsibility. Failure can make you feel as though life has ground to a halt, and that can lead to aggression, depression, anxiety, uncertainty. Most people aren't as successful as they want to be because they've let negativity eat into their life. You need to take responsibility for everything you do. You have one chance before life catches you up and stares at you in the mirror. And there is nothing worse than looking back with regret, wishing you took the chances while you had the opportunity. Don't live with regret.

Life can be beautiful. How beautiful it is to wake and see the sunshine. And even if it's raining, you've still woken to another day of your life. People with disabilities might not be able to walk outside and feel the rain or the sun. People with terminal illnesses don't have the same choice you have. Those disadvantaged souls are dependent on others to make things possible for them. You have a choice: you have the ability to create change. Life has so many moving parts. Every day is a new day with new challenges. Tell yourself: I'm going to have a good day, I'm going to set new goals, I'm going to achieve those goals, I'm going to be strong, I'm going to be a success. Create and take those opportunities while you can. Life has meaning – never take it for granted.

On this journey of life, you're going to face significant failure, significant challenges. If you don't love your life, then make the change happen. You have the power to. Your life is your life, and you have the right to live it the best way you can. You have to have self-discipline and take full responsibility and control. Run towards your dreams and ambitions; never run away from them. Understand that life has meaning, that you do have a purpose, that your life does have reason.

✳✳✳

You've got to remove negativity from your journey, convince yourself you are worthy and set your frequency to a positive place. Life does have a gift – a gift of giving you what you wish for – you just need to set your sights on finding it. Find your focus and follow your dreams: they can be reached. One thing I realised was that I was spending too much time on my phone, scrolling through social media, analysing everybody else's lives and how successful they were, watching weight training videos with people in fantastic shape, seeing people driving their super-fast cars. It seems everybody in today's society wants to be a social media celebrity. I think it's great to share positivity – true, not fake, positivity. So, I reduced my time on social media to maybe an hour or two per day, to coach my mind away from the fake images. I do believe too much social media drains the goodness from your mind.

For almost two years now, I haven't watched the news. Since losing my mother, and others, I have surrounded myself with positive images and positive sounds and visions. News is always so negative and it would affect me; just reading about anything traumatic would send me to a dark place. When I watch any television now, it's documentaries or something upbeat.

Excess social media made me anxious and depressed. I found the less I spent on my mobile phone, the more alert I became. I started reading and watching positive things that uplifted my energy. Without negative stimulation, my attention span grew stronger, I had more ideas and I became more creative. Unnecessary distractions simply drain your ability to focus on the positive. My own research over the last two years, including clinical trials I have followed, has proved how much mental damage social media platforms can do. Overstimulation creates chemical imbalances within the brain.

Regulate how much time you spend on social media. Stop looking at your phone every second of the day. Stop comparing your life with everybody else's. We spend far too much time on Facebook – TikTok – YouTube. Try restricting your time to thirty minutes per day. If you do use social media, look at something positive, something motivational, something happy. When you do, the chemical balance becomes levelled, rather than overstimulated. There's only one reason and one reason alone why people find the need to scroll away for hours: boredom.

Children nowadays suffer more mental health issues than ever. Growing up in a social media world, where acceptance is a must and there's online bullying, is mentally damaging. Kids have even taken their lives because of what happens on social media. Programming positivity is vital in those younger years. I failed to focus on anything positive when I was a kid, and that was during the seventies, *without* the internet.

Humans cannot be happy one hundred per cent of the time. We will always face obstacles – that's part and parcel of life. But we do have the ability to change the direction. We will all have low moments, we will all suffer setbacks, we will all get caught up in things we shouldn't, and we will all lose our way at one time or another. If you wish to stay lost, then lost you will stay. However, you do have a choice. And choice starts within your own mind. Think "mind over matter".

Here are some examples to get you back on track.

Number one: write down your reason. I found writing down my thoughts was far more powerful than thinking them. It's a great way to start getting real focus.

Number two: realise life is short. We are only on this earth for a very short space of time. Don't get old and live with the regret of not taking the chances while you had them. I lost a very beautiful friend, my lovely friend Jan, to cancer. As I held her hand, she said to me, "I wish I could turn back the clock and do all the things I could have done." Jan was only seventy years old, and though that's not old by today's standards, those opportunities had passed. You only get one shot. So, don't sit and wait for things to happen – focus on the things you love and go get them.

Number three: feed your mind with positivity. Keep social media to a limit and don't waste hours on useless information. There are so many ways to feed your mind with positivity: go for lovely walks in the countryside or around your local park while listening to happy music. Coach your mind to consume happiness, which will, in turn, lift your vibrational frequency to a much stronger place. Think about self-development: focus on you and you alone, seek to learn and grow. This will create positivity in all areas of your life. Practise gratitude and appreciate who you are and who you can be. There is no more powerful force on earth than gratitude. If you practise it every day, you will grow stronger by the day.

Number four: keep moving. Regardless of your age, whether you're twenty-one or eighty, activity is great for the body and mind. Go for walks, swim, get on the treadmill. I have spent over thirty-seven years weight training. I found when I didn't weight train or do any fitness, I became lethargic and my motivation levels dropped dramatically. Every form of fitness stimulates the brain and releases endorphins. Physical exercise at whatever level you choose is a great way to freshen the mind and stay motivated. It improves your focus and can lower anxiety, ease depression and reduce stress levels. Even your posture can affect your mental state. If you tend to slump over your desk, draw your shoulders back and be aware of how you're sitting (and standing too).

Last but not least, number five: know what you want from life. Goals are essential. Without goals, there is no reason; without reason, there are no goals. Goals define where you go in life; goals determine your outcome; goals keep you on track. Science as well as common sense shows that you are much more likely to enjoy success if you have clearly defined goals than someone who doesn't. Be very specific with your goals and what you want from them. Again, write them down. See them on paper. Set realistic time limits to achieve them. Make your goals meaningful to get your life back on track. You don't have to stay in the same position for the rest of your life.

✱✱✱

Sometimes, I would wake extremely tired, even after a deep sleep. I was tired of myself, bored of my existence. After my counselling with Julie, I started going to my mother's grave every day to apologise for the son I was. I couldn't change the past, but I decided I could no longer live in it. I couldn't bring back my loved ones. Little Lyrah, just nine years old, lost her battle with an inoperable brain tumour and this beat my soul into a dark place. I didn't believe I would ever return from that place, but I did. The loss was devastating. One day, there will be a cure for that tumour.

What I am trying to say here is, though I couldn't change the past, I could change tomorrow. I had to make a decision to either stay in one place and relive my trauma every day for the rest of my life or open a new chapter and live my life positively. None of us can afford to let our past dictate our future. Life is controlled by our emotions, good and bad. I didn't want to wait until I possibly felt strong enough. I had to make that change there and then. There is no point in waiting for things to happen: you have to grab life with both hands. Self-discipline is essential – you won't be able to focus without it. Ask yourself whether you practise self-discipline. Take a moment to assess your life and construct your belief system. A little quote: "The quieter you become, the more you are able to hear." Take time for you.

It's truly hard to be happy if you're not being yourself, and most of us have no clue who we are at times. If you focus on the past too much, and you constantly analyse what's missing from your life, you could become anxious and depressed. It's easy to look for those missing pieces of your jigsaw puzzle by scrolling on your mobile phone to see how others are living their lives.

During my darkest days, the mental health team wanted to put me on heavy medication. Plenty of people will require medication, but I believe society depends far too much on it. It masks why you're feeling what you're feeling. For me, medication was not the answer. It muffled my motivation and it stole away my focus, so I withdrew from taking it.

Drinking tons of caffeine is not the answer either. Any stimulant – cannabis, alcohol – is not the answer. I know people who use recreational drugs just to get through the day. I was one of them once. I didn't recognise why I needed drugs to have a happy day. I have been alcohol- and drug-free for quite some time now and I refuse to be around people who use drugs. Alcohol is a much more socially acceptable fix; however, I don't want to be around people who rely on drugs, because they don't vibrate happy energy to my frequency. In my experience, you will never succeed in life if you take drugs of any kind, on any level, or drink heavily. You won't be able to focus on anything other than the next drink or the next fix just to feel normal.

Later in the book, I will touch on the amazing benefits of meditation. Calming the mind is a terrific way to learn how to focus. You can reprogramme your mind. When you've read this book, take stock. If you are already in a happy place and have realised your goals and ambitions, then well done – you may not realise it, but people will have thrived off your positivity. But if you have suffered trauma, and aren't in a happy place, take a moment to address what happened to you. Is there anything from your childhood that could have determined your outcome in adulthood? My childhood certainly dictated my outcome, which almost cost me my life.

✳✳✳

Focus on yourself, lay your past to rest – you can't rewrite it. Learn to manage your mind. Withdraw any negative thoughts and don't overthink things that haven't even happened. Take control of your consciousness: you have the power to create positive thoughts.

Why think negative thoughts when you can give the same amount of attention to positive ones? What an amazing way of conditioning your mind – always thinking about the best possible outcomes. What a great way to live your life. Be conscious of what's going on in your thoughts and start paying attention to yourself, your emotions and your actions.

Check on your thoughts, even when you're filling up your car or doing your shopping. What are they saying? Replace any negative thoughts with positive ones. Even if you have to close your eyes to do it, think about that positive thought deeply. Say it to yourself and be aware that the little voice in the back of your mind may well direct the negative thought back.

The more I used visualisation, the more everything I focused on seemed to fall into place. After fifty-two years, I had finally found the cure for negativity. I embraced the success in that, and my inner wealth grew. When I talk about success, I talk about living a life of happiness – to be able to focus on something and achieve it. For the first time in my life, I have found my way. It would be amazing if we could work this out in our younger days, but that's not how life works. We have to experience life's upsets and losses to gain wisdom, achieve knowledge and move forward in a positive way.

Many people never find their true potential in life, which is so tragic. They're quite happy to simply exist. I never ever wanted to just exist. I wanted success but I took many wrong paths to find it. There is no quick and easy solution: you have to work at it. Nothing is going to land on your plate just like that.

I know how it might sound, but trust me, my discovery of the power of the universe and its level of energy has enabled me to focus with clarity. It's beautiful and unbelievable. I cannot express enough how vital it is to tune yourself into a stronger vibrational frequency. I was unable to focus on anything positive, because everything I tried, I failed at. Time and time again.

I now set my alarm at 6:30 a.m. whether it's summer or winter. I wake up bright and early to take on my day with a fresh, cleansed mind. I tell myself I'm going to have a great day. I don't look at social media or use a device for two hours before and after bedtime. I check my messages because I run my own charitable organisation, but that's it. I strive to get up early and go to bed at a sensible time to get a good night's sleep. This regulates my mood and stabilises my mind. I always make sure I eat a breakfast of protein and carbohydrates within thirty minutes of getting out of bed. Food is a great mood changer. Skipping breakfast can affect your emotional health.

Design and structure your day. Set achievable goals – ones you're unlikely to fail on. Create small positive habits. All of this helped me along my journey, and I hope someone else can learn from my wisdom. To come from being suicidal to writing my second book, the results are clear: I am very much alive and stronger than ever.

Here is a quote I live by:

"Always remember your focus determines your reality. Focus less on your weaknesses and more on your strengths. Take time to believe in yourself and the universe will be forced to believe in you."

— *GEORGE LUCAS*

Chapter 3

Nikola Tesla – 'The Genius'

You are probably wondering why I'm writing a chapter on Nikola Tesla. I will enlighten your curiosity. I've spoken about vibrational frequency and the importance of its connection with the universe. When it comes to vibrational frequency, Nikola Tesla was a genius. Nicknamed the 'Master of Lightning', Tesla wished to give the world an unlimited supply of energy. I became fascinated with him, and for around two years I have researched this amazing man in detail.

Throughout my counselling I discovered an energy which I had never known existed. The positive energy from my sessions gave me such a spiritual lift – far more than simply talking about my troubles. Yes, it was a therapeutic way of seeking a healthier mind, but I'm talking about something much deeper here. I began to look on the internet to learn more about this amazing energy I was feeling. I read views on personal vibrational frequency and how if we tune ourselves into the universe, we attract people to vibe from our positive energy.

This is where I kept coming across Tesla. He inspired me beyond all words, changing the world with electricity. You're probably thinking what has electricity and vibrational energy got to do with feeling good. I shall tell you.

Tesla was a technological visionary: he could envision great things and make them work. Tesla's father, a priest, taught him how to read people's minds and repeat long passages of verse. Tesla would have visions with strong flashes of light, with no understanding of what they were. These bright lights and visions were just the start.

Fascinated by the beauty of Niagara Falls, he imagined a huge wheel run by waterfalls to create energy. This is just one example of how his mind was thinking at such a young age. Tesla invented from that vision three 5,000 horsepower water turbine generators. This is the extent of the true potential of our minds.

✳✳✳

After almost losing his life to a serious illness, Tesla started to study engineering. He became obsessed with the science of electricity. Every spark created a thousand echoes within his amazing brain. His visions were ridiculed by inventors. This amazing visionary was so far ahead of his time many failed to vibe his energy and creations.

Tesla would take long walks in the city parks, and one afternoon when the sun was just setting, he was reminded of a passage he'd once read: *The glow retreats, done is the day of toil, it yonder hastes, new fields of life exploring; ah, that no wing can lift me from the soil, upon its track to follow, follow soaring!* This was the beginning for him – this amazing gift of light from the sun setting, the flash of its energy, the vibrations passing like bolts of lightning through his mind. It was a vision, and these visions became more apparent and regular thereafter.

The power of his mind was visualisation – he could see things all moving and working. Tesla had a further amazing vision of transmitting and receiving energy without connecting wires. How can any energy be transmitted without physical connectivity? This is where the story really begins. I call it the 'higher power'.

Tesla experimented with high-frequency electricity. In 1873, James Clerk Maxwell had mathematically proven that light, for example the sun, is electromagnetic radiation vibrating at an extremely high frequency. Tesla explored this energy and went on to invent the Tesla coil, which operated at and, in turn, transmitted a very high frequency. He would invite people to test his theories by having electricity pass through their bodies to light a lamp. With high frequencies, Tesla developed some of the first neon illuminations, and X-ray photographs, a discovery that came about while holding a wireless, illuminated vacuum tube. This was the birth of wireless energy transmission – transmitting a frequency without visible connectivity. Radio transmission was made possible via radio antenna, an invisible connection made between two frequencies on the same wavelength.

This transmitting energy without physical connectivity really intrigued me. It felt more mystical than science. It opened the doors to whether human beings could communicate telepathically when tuned to high frequency brain waves. This is where Tesla had an astonishing vision, a truly disturbing one. He saw clouds, with angels all around, one of whom had his mother's features. That instant, he felt certain his mother had died. He couldn't explain it, but sure enough, she had. Tesla was convinced he and his mother were tuned to the same vibrational frequency. Tesla explored this vision of his mother in depth. On one occasion, he held a coil, tuned to his body, and collected energy from the room without a visible connection. This energy would run motors and create light and so on. Further discovery showed that Tesla coils would transmit and receive powerful radio signals when tuned together on the same frequency.

This is where cosmic waves came into play. From time to time, Tesla would apply electricity to his body, to give him life force. He believed it gave him strong, mindful energy as well as a deeper interest and exploration of Eastern thought and spiritualism. He became inspired by a Hindu teacher called Swami Vivekananda and began to look at the universe as a symphony of vibrations and waves. The power of the universe, with all that moves and spins, has vibrational energy. Everywhere, there is energy. And so Tesla decided to experiment. In 1898, he attached a small mechanical oscillator to an iron pillar with precisely timed pulses, which caused the whole building he was in to vibrate. Tesla was obsessed with vibrational frequency and resonance. What he discovered was, with the right frequency, one can move the world.

Lightning, for example, transmits energy from one place to another via electric signals, with no wires – just electricity conducting energy. During one of his experiments, Tesla created his own lightning with an antenna. One evening, the antenna started to receive signals, which he believed to be extraterrestrial communication. The message that was sent was the numbers 1, 2, 3. Tesla was ridiculed for this message from outer space. Yet, even today, unexplainable signals are recorded from space – and, in some cases, the evidence covered up. But this proved that something is out there. It's thought these signals are transmitted from the sun, as well as being the stars' electrical pulses from another energy source.

Tesla's discovery of the power of the sun was so beautiful – all this powerful energy resonating from a single source: the sun. When the sun shines, we automatically feel good. It lifts our spirits. The sun is energy in tune with the moon and the stars. Tesla, in my opinion, was a messenger of energy. For the late 1800s, his visualisation was years ahead of his time.

Tesla discovered a way of harnessing the sun's energy. Life craves energy. Why do we feel so down when we don't see the sun? All default responses are energy-saving reactions: how can we gain more energy? How can we raise our consciousness and increase our intelligence? According to Tesla, more energy means higher levels of operating power for our consciousness. If you apply time to this equation, it means the longer we sustain higher levels of energy for our consciousness, the more intelligence we download from the universe, and the more intelligence we integrate into our being.

So, what is the source of our energy? Where does the power come from? What is the spring that drives all? We see the ocean rise and fall, the rivers flow along with the wind, and the rain beating upon our windows. We see trains arrive and depart, cars and motorbikes, transportation and movement. We hear the voices of people walking by. We feel, we smell, we touch, we taste. Think about all this movement around us, all this energy being created. This all stems from one single source: the sun. The sun is the power that drives all: the sun supplies all human energy and maintains all human life. How do we increase human energy? To increase our energy and vibrational frequency, we have to think in terms of speed. Food is just processed sunlight. For photosynthesis to take place, plants need carbon dioxide, water and light. Fruit, vegetables, meat – everything we eat – creates energy. The energy we consume is the same as the light energy plants use for photosynthesis. Tesla's form of energy gives us energy similar to the sun's rays.

✳✳✳

Our birth is connected to the circles of the solar system. If you were to live until you were eighty-four, you would have completed seven solar cycles and one thousand and eight solar cycles. The ancient religions noted the sun to be one of the most profound energies of the universe. The sound of the sun cannot be heard by the human ear, but if it could, it would be just how the ancient Hindus told it. It is a mantra that can be entwined with human speech, which is why when I wake in the morning, I pray out loud to the sun. I send my vibrational frequency to the universe to energise it. I believe prayer needs to be vibrational and spoken out loud. There is a strong bond between our planet and us, and the material things around us, which are vibrating together.

Ancient Greek philosopher Pythagoras described the sound of the sun as a deep, humming sound. Question is, how did the ancient Hindus know of this deep, humming sound? Note Hindus also give a deep 'Om' when they recite spiritual texts.

✳✳✳

Tesla always stated if you wish to find out the secrets of the universe, think in terms of energy and frequency and vibrations. We have the power to achieve anything – the universe is our classroom. Tesla opened my mind. I have been so inspired by him because he, too, began to embrace the spiritual side of life and its purpose. I hope this brings a little understanding, a little vision, like it has me. If you activate your third eye, you will enjoy clarity. For me, meditation is what gives me clarity.

✳✳✳

Tesla had a theory of the magic of the numbers 3 – 6 – 9 and how they relate to the third eye. Their magic guided my third eye to embrace the energy of the universe. The number in tantra is 369, and tantra also sees the universe as a vibrating frequency. This was Tesla's idea of everything being vibration, energy and frequency.

Number 3 signs are the three states of consciousness: the waking state, *jagrat*; the dreaming state, *swapna*; and the dark sleep we go into, or the void, *sushupti*. These three states are the three suns of our bodies. The lower sun, we need to shut down – the biological mind. The next sun is the neural cortex – the chattering mind. And the third sun is the third eye – the sun of the heart and the head. Once open, the third eye gives us access to thousands of suns that bring light and clarity. Then there is the fourth state of consciousness, *turiya*. This is where you get to design your reality.

Number 6 is the number of chakras we count to obtain access to the third eye. The five elements are: earth, water, fire, air and space. The sixth chakra is known as the third eye chakra. Its purpose is pattern recognition, or the "seeing chakra". The element of the third eye is light, which enables us to take in the shape and form of things around us from a distance.

Number 9 is the number of levels you have to climb to leave your body. There are nine openings in your body: two in the lower half of your body, two nostrils, two eyes, two ears and one mouth. The tenth gate is at the top of the head, to open up the third eye and give you access to the divine consciousness above.

Tesla believed 369 was the secret code of the universe and that it belonged to a higher dimensional world. According to Tesla, 3 – 6 – 9 were sacred numbers and if you took note, you would see them in your daily life. The universe is mathematical. Almost everything in nature is symmetrical and follows a geometric pattern. Tesla would create mathematical sequences and every time he did, 3 – 6 – 9 would be missing. Many mathematical paths were taken to test this theory and, each time, 3 – 6 – 9 wouldn't be there.

People practise the 369 manifestation method to lift their vibrational frequencies and become more successful. When I was writing *My Tormented Mind*, I learned very quickly that writing my thoughts down on paper supercharged my intention to write about my life. To this day, if I wake with low energy, I will write down my manifestation of the day. I write in the present tense. I use an adjective to describe that feeling. I then visualise how amazing that manifestation would feel. I act as if it's already happened. Have faith in yourself and your mind won't doubt your intentions. Once I have written my manifestation, I then look at the sky and the sun – since the sun is my god of energy – and say it out loud. Words are a vibration and once you say them, you remove doubt. I do this for seventeen seconds, to ignite my vibrational energy.

Here is one of my manifestations: "I will have a great day today and make sure all those around me smile, and that my whole day is blessed with bright energy and happiness. Thank you for the beautiful sunshine and universe."

On days I feel low I write this down three times, feeling the energy as I do. I then repeat my manifestation six times, like I believe it every single time. Then, before bed, I will write down my manifestation nine times on the same sheet of paper and repeat it nine times. Your affirmations will then be the last thing on your mind before you go to sleep. The 369 method sends out such a strong vibration into the universe and programmes your mind to your affirmation, which keeps you aligned with the universe. I use this method when I feel low or people have drained my energy levels. I regain positivity by reprogramming my energy into the universe.

✳✳✳

I have questioned life and my identity. My own experiences have shown me who I am, why I'm here and what my purpose is on earth. Programming your subconscious mind, your thoughts and your words is so very powerful. Even talking to yourself is powerful. Mind and matter are co-related. Your mind will influence your outcomes.

I have turned all my trauma into a new reality, and you can learn to create a new future too.

Wherever you place your attention, you place your energy. Combine clear intentions with emotions, to amplify the energy field around you. When your energy becomes more positive, learn to feel abundance before you feel wealth – in all aspects of your life. Everything is energy, and you need to learn how to manipulate the energy around you. Create and visualise. You are here for a reason. You are blessed with the most precious gift: the gift of life.

I wish to embrace Nikola Tesla and thank him for showing me the light. Tesla was convinced there is a higher power – something out there feeding us information, driving our energy. Tesla, Thomas Edison, Albert Einstein, Elon Musk – where do these remarkable humans with their incredible foresight get their inspiration from? There are many other inspirational people, but through Tesla, I gained so much awareness of my own energy. He helped me open my third eye and look at life in such a way I would receive insight into vibrational frequency.

✳✳✳

"If you want to find the secrets of the universe, think in terms of energy, frequency and vibration. Though free to think and act, we are all held together, like the stars in the firmament, with ties inseparable. These ties cannot be seen, but we can feel them. For ages this idea has been proclaimed in the consummately wise teachings of religion, probably not alone as a means of ensuring peace and humanity among men, but as a deeply founded truth. The Buddhist expresses it in one way, Christianity in another, but both say the same: 'We are all one.'"

— *NIKOLA TESLA*

Chapter 4

Spiritual Meditation

I never fully really understood the word 'spiritual', other than it being something beautiful we can't see. As children, we don't really understand spiritual belief. My mother would share both her religious and her spiritual beliefs with me, with the magical thought that there was a higher power looking over and protecting us. I would pray to Jesus, especially when I was naughty, and pray for forgiveness. I never really thought about religion or spirituality, not until I lost my father at the age of twenty-two. And that's when my life took a turn for the worse.

I lost all respect for faith and religion. I became a very lost soul, got addicted to drugs and ended up in prison. I was in emotional turmoil, and the journey I was on was one of utter destruction – emotional and physical.

From the age of twenty-two to fifty-one, I had no direction or purpose. Losing my mother so tragically took me to a point of no return. I went back to drink and drugs. I'd drink when I woke up, I'd drink during the day, I'd drink in the evening and I'd drink into the early hours of the morning. My body couldn't take any more, and when my mother died, part of my soul died with her. On 13 January 2021, I was rushed into hospital, after a half-hearted attempt to end my life.

While lying in that hospital bed, with my mother just corridors away in the mortuary, I questioned my life and my purpose. I'd tasted death. I could smell it around me. Where do you go when death calls you? On 17 February 2021, my mother was laid to rest. Watching her being lowered into the ground where my father was buried was so painful. My heart, my soul, my entire being were laid to rest that day.

I was blessed to have some wonderful friends hold me up. One of them recommended I look into private counselling and offered to pay for it. I was introduced to a lady named Julie Lucas. On our first meeting, I immediately felt safe. My counselling wouldn't take place in an office, but in a lovely summer house in her garden.

Julie asked if I would consider meditation. This was something I had never looked into before, but I was willing to give it a try as I knew I needed to dig deep to open doors that had been firmly closed for many years. I was a little bit afraid, though I wasn't sure why. I think it was the unknown that frightened me – where it was going to take me. But Julie made me feel relaxed. All I could hear were the birds, and at one point a butterfly flew in through the double doors, as if it was an angel telling me it was going to be OK. It was incredibly beautiful and incredibly meaningful.

During my meditation I was told to completely relax and to feel the energy in my feet. Julie asked me to tense them and then release the pressure, and to use the same process through my calves into my thighs, then in my back, through my arms into my hands and in my shoulders. Pushing the pressure from the ground up and then releasing it was amazing. I found the breathing incredibly beneficial too – breathing in for four seconds, holding for four seconds, and breathing out for four seconds. It felt peaceful.

Julie said we were going to try visualisation and then asked me a series of questions. She asked me to look for myself as a child. I looked over to the corner of a room and saw a little boy of about seven years old. He was sitting with his legs crossed, with his arms around his knees and his head face down, as if he was crying. It was as though I had been locked in a very dark room since the age of seven, afraid, frightened, lost. This little boy had been there for over forty years.

Julie then asked me to hold out my hand to him. The little boy raised his head and held out his hand. By offering him safety, our two souls reunited and became one. With that, my child image stood up. Julie then gently asked me to look towards a bright light. I took my child hand and, on her instruction, took a deep breath and led my child self into the light. My heart was racing, my fists were clenched and I began to cry. The dark spirit within my child's mind was about to be released.

There was a force of energy I can't fully explain. The light gave me a feeling of what I had missed as a child. It was just so kind, so loving, like a cuddle from God himself, welcoming me and my newly reunited souls. I'd finally been reunited with my childhood. The personal vibrational frequency I received that day was beautiful beyond words. The energy was electric. Love was shining bright like summer sunshine. I had arrived, reborn and cleansed of hatred. This was meditation beyond spirituality.

Julie roused me from my meditation and wiped the tears from my eyes. The only way I can explain how I felt it is that the energy came from a higher power. I left that counselling session knowing this was the beginning of another life.

Some days later, I returned to my memorial bench at the beautiful Aylesford Priory. As I approached it, to my complete surprise, I saw a plaque placed where the original would have once been. Throughout the months of me sitting on that bench, there'd never been a plaque. You could call this coincidence, but I don't. 'Shirley B: To an amazing mother, so dearly missed and loved. An angel of life that has touched so many hearts.'

It was a message, a strong message. I strongly believed I had a spiritual connection with that bench as I too had had no identity. At that very moment, my energy soared. I gently caressed the plaque with my thumb to say thank you to Shirley B for listening to my troubles all those months. Not only had I found my identity, but the beautiful Shirley B had revealed hers.

To this very day, every week I visit Shirley B. I sit and I meditate, out loud, with the intention to send out love, strength and, most of all, gratitude. Since that day, it's as if the very last piece of the jigsaw puzzle has fit into place. It inspired me to write my feelings down on paper so I could see them, which then inspired me to write a book about my journey.

***

Discovering spiritual meditation has been my lifesaver. I am so grateful to Julie for introducing me to it. I have looked deeper into meditation and found ways of taking my inner energy and blessing it with a frequency that is far stronger than anything I have ever known. I use spiritual meditation to connect to a divine higher power. Religions such as Hinduism, Judaism, Buddhism and Christianity touch on loving kindness and tranquillity and finding inner peace – the most vital aspect of spiritual meditation – as well as connection to the universe and its higher powers.

Whatever spiritual meditation you practise, finding the desire to connect with the higher power of the universe – God, your higher self, your inner self – is a must. Unlike other forms of meditation, spiritual meditation is more than stress reduction or relaxation. The intention to connect to something greater than yourself is what makes the practice spiritual. In my experience, spirituality comes from the connection to one's soul. This form of meditation is highly individual.

I'm a believer that if you don't feel an automatic connection to something deep, or you feel nothing at all, you shouldn't force it. With any type of meditation, the more you try, the harder it will be to achieve a meditative state. If you are just getting into spiritual meditation, I recommend staying away from conversations about spiritual meditation practice. Everybody's experiences will differ, and, as a novice, you may be misguided. We are all unique, and our discoveries and journeys will all be unique too. Everybody is different; however, we're striving for the same result: peace.

***

Meditation gives me the courage to do everything with great intention. It gives me a stronger vibrational frequency to both deliver and attract positivity in all areas of my life, from relationships to work. Meditation has benefited me in such a beautiful way.

I find I don't need to meditate every day, but you'll have to find what works for you. I practise, at the most, twice a week to relieve any negativity from my mind and draw positivity from the universe. If you suffer from depression, anxiety or stress, meditation could be really beneficial for you. And for children with those conditions too.

I now have a beautiful level of confidence and identity. Expressing confidence is a great frequency to give out to the universe. Everything around us vibrates, and everything around you will pick up on your frequency. When I say everything, I mean everything – from your kitchen table to your car, from the walls within your home to the cat, the dog, everything. When you find the real you, you'll find life will be a lot more manageable. My sleep became deeper, when the rumbled confusion in my mind was no longer there every night. Anxiety, stress and depression elevate lack of sleep, and we all know how draining lack of sleep is.

Here is one method I wish to share with you. Place your hands in a comfortable position on your body and start to connect with your breath the same way you do during your meditation practice. This will help relax the body and release whatever is keeping you up at night. Simply focus on your breath. This calms the mind and body, which aids sleep.

✳✳✳

There are many ways to meditate. When I was first told about meditation, I envisaged sitting on the floor cross-legged, hands on both knees, breathing in and out. I didn't want to try that. Why? Simply because, when you reach your mid-fifties, the knees and joints are not as flexible as they once were.

One form of meditation which has worked for me goes like this: place your right hand over your heart centre, your left hand just underneath your belly button, then close your eyes. Start to listen to your breath and connect with it. Listen to what it sounds like. Feel it, as your body moves with every breath. Allow your breath to flow at a comfortable pace. Imagine a light inside of you. Visualise the colour and brightness. Feel the temperature of that light. Walk into the light to guide you to a place of peace and higher power. This is close to the method Julie used to take my childhood image into that great light. Once you are in that light, absorbing its colour and its radiance, you will feel the power of its energy.

Once you feel comfortable with the light, start to follow it as it moves out of your body and into the sky. Follow it as it moves through the clouds and into the heavens. Allow yourself to feel safe and connected. Explore and feel open to whatever may come to you. When you're ready, bring your light back down into your body, start to come back to the present moment, wiggle your fingers and toes and then gently open your eyes as you slowly come out of your meditation. I find this incredibly beneficial.

Here's another method. Find yourself a comfortable seated position so that your wrists and ankles aren't crossed and your back is upright and not leaning on anything. Make sure you won't be disturbed and you're in a quiet place with no distractions, mobile phones or music, or even the sound of traffic. Begin by observing the rhythm of your breathing. As you become more tuned into your breathing, allow your awareness to tune into your heart rate. Feel the rhythm of your heartbeat. (It's OK if your mind gets busy. This is normal and will clear once you are deeper into your meditation.) Thank your ego for its input and then let it know it can rest. Now let your awareness move into your heart space and simply observe how you feel there. It is a welcoming space, a peaceful space, a place of tranquillity. Make sure you feel safe and happy being there. If there is any resistance, remove it. When you feel ready, allow your awareness to focus back on your heartbeat, then your breathing. Return to the room and open your eyes. This is a quick but calming process for when you are having a busy day and just need a moment of clarity.

I've been asked when and where is the best time to meditate. The answer to that is, any time. I like meditating in the morning or in the evening. Meditating in nature is most beneficial for me. I tune into the sounds of the birds and listen to the world around me, which is why I normally head to the Chatham Naval Memorial in Gillingham. It's at the top of a hill and very rarely, early morning, do you find many people there. I have my little spot where the sun can shine on me while I meditate. If I have a spiritual connection with a place, I will meditate there.

Plenty of people prefer meditating in the comfort of their own home, which I also do. When I meditated with Julie, it was during the summer months, and we sat in her summer house surrounded by the voices of nature. It's important for anyone looking into meditation to find their place of peace, whether that be outside or in the comfort of their home. Finding your place is paramount to successful meditation.

You can meditate with crystals and stones, ancient pieces that provide an earthly connection. Crystals have been used in healing and meditation for thousands of years, which begs the question: do crystals have healing powers? I believe they do. I carry around certain crystals and stones for energy and protection. For crystal meditation, you'll need your chosen crystal and a willingness to practise, particularly if meditation is new for you. I have practised with stones. I have them around my home and find them truly energising. I was given a pebble – yes, a simple pebble from a beach – painted with a beautiful butterfly. I immediately connected with that pebble, and I touch it every night for energy, peacefulness and safety. I also kiss my mother's and my father's photos and wish all my loved ones goodnight. I find peace in that. The art of all these experiences is that if you find comfort in something – regardless of what other people think – that can only be a good thing.

I want to touch on grounding and learning to connect yourself to a higher level. To ground yourself and ask your highest self and the highest beings to help you in your session, set your intention that any information or actions are for the greatest good of humanity. If you have your chosen crystal, ask it for permission to use its vibrations. Simply connect to your intuition and feel for an answer. Connect to your breath and the crystal vibrations, keep your breath relaxed, and see where the energies take you. Some people like to shut their eyes; some prefer to keep them open. When I experimented with this, I found closing my eyes worked better. With meditation, I occasionally have distracting thoughts, which by all accounts is common. If the thoughts are negative, I'll normally acknowledge them and send them away. If they don't go away, what I then do is say them out loud to send my vibration out there and remove the negativity. The trick in every form of meditation is to eliminate those stray thoughts, to let them pass through your mind without you grabbing hold of them.

It's recommended the crystals remain in your hand for no more than twenty minutes. If at any time you feel uncomfortable with the crystals, put them down and drink a glass of water. If you don't want to touch the crystals while you meditate, you can create a crystal grid or a circle. Place your crystals in a sacred shape around you or directly in front of you to focus on during your meditation.

I really like having candles in my meditation. Lit candles make me feel still and help me enter a beautiful state of mind. I love candles while meditating in the bath. The combination of light and hot water warms my soul. These are just a couple of ideas if you're struggling to meditate in your living room or somewhere away from home.

✳✳✳

If you are reaching into using crystals, here are some examples and their benefits.

- Amethyst has a strong healing energy, which aids sleep and supports blood circulation and balance.

- Garnet crystals can be beneficial for providing energy and regeneration. Garnet is considered a good choice when recovering from illness.

- Quartz: there are many kinds of quartz crystal, from clear to rose to smoky. Clear quartz is believed to improve awareness and reduce stress. Rose quartz, my favourite crystal of all, is known as the crystal of unconditional love. It boosts self-love and loving relationships with others. Smoky quartz is a grounding stone and may help you feel rooted to the planet. It's also believed to lift mood and protect.

- Black tourmaline is said to protect against mobile phone radiation, though there's no evidence to support this. Tourmaline is generally believed to protect from even the greatest of negative energies.

- Selenite is commonly used in both meditation and mediation. It is said to help the person meditating connect to a higher consciousness.

- Citrine attracts joy and abundance.

- Sodalite is believed to bring order to your mind.

- Lapis lazuli boosts spiritual development and can increase your intuitive abilities and resolve conflict.

- Tiger's eye is known to support during times of change. It empowers you to be assertive and find clarity in your intentions.

***

There are other avenues of meditation which I am yet to discover, one of which is walking meditation. This involves focusing on your stride and movement rather than your breath. Walking the labyrinth is a centuries-old practice of contemplation. When you walk through a labyrinth, you follow the path as it winds its way towards the centre. You take a moment to pause when you reach the centre, before turning and exiting via the same path you came in on. Labyrinth walking has its root in spiritual and meditative practice.

Meditation helps people from all walks of life. I hope this chapter gives you some idea of where it can take you.

"Meditation is a sort of prayer. The highest meditation is to think of nothing. If you remain without thoughts, great power will come."

— *SWAMI VIVEKANANDA*

Chapter 5

The Meaning of Life

The meaning of life – what is that? The meaning of life, as I see it now, is one word: happiness. Happiness in whatever form that comes. Being happy is the only medication you will ever need for your mind.

As a child, I never understood the meaning of love. I knew how to show love; however, I never really received much in the way of love. I found love came with conditions. The whole world of love was lost to me, and this resulted in failed relationships. This was a knock-on effect of living a confused life right from birth. Maybe it was a seventies thing. Maybe there are thousands, if not millions, of lost souls who can't give reason as to why they became the people they became – especially those born before the eighties, when life was not explained but lived. If you have had a blessed journey, you then possibly won't be asking these questions.

Counselling was a refreshing open door to a soul that failed to understand life. I began to understand the meaning of love, to see it as unconditional. Happiness and unconditional love are the two main ingredients for a blessed journey. I've always taken the time to care for others and despite previously believing my frequency to be low, I still found the energy to give without wanting to receive. Because I never really understood how to recognise love, I couldn't receive it, and therefore the majority of what I tried to love failed. Within this chemistry of misunderstanding, I was still able to give what I believed to be a positive vibrational energy, yet the signals were wrong. Like hiding behind a false smile.

I have been running a charitable organisation for almost eight years now: Bring Every Kind Smile (BEKS). We help bring smiles to those less fortunate in life, from very sick children to the elderly. We take them for a day at the seaside. Just for a smile. Bringing a smile to a terminally ill child and their family is magical. It gives me inner wealth and the energy I receive in return makes me smile. When you are battling to smile yourself, it is truly uplifting to receive such positive vibrational energy and focus. Many of us don't realise the effect we have on other people's lives. For me, smiling is incredibly infectious and seeing poorly children smile answered all the questions I had unanswered.

Helping others less fortunate than myself, combined with unconditional love, is what I call the true meaning of life. It brings me happiness. What an amazing gift of gratitude you can give yourself to find your own meaning of life. Discovering this has given purpose to my existence: I wake up every day wanting to help those in need. I have held the hands of children I fundraised for who lost their battle for life. I have attended their funerals and kissed them goodbye. The energy from knowing I made them smile and created memories for their families comes from a place that exceeds all emotion. For me, the meaning of life is giving and loving unconditionally. You have to find your own meaning of life. We are unique human beings with unique identities.

The search for the meaning of life leads people and cultures to believe different things. We can dig deep here and investigate scientific inquiry about existence, social ties, consciousness and happiness. We can look into symbolic meanings, purpose, ethical values, good and evil, free will, and God and the afterlife, but I suppose no one can define the meaning of life.

Some people believe we, as humankind, are the creation of a supernatural entity called God; that God had an intelligent purpose in creating us and that this intelligent purpose is the meaning of life. I don't propose to rehearse the well-worn arguments for and against the existence of God, but even if God exists and even if he had an intelligent purpose in creating us, no one really knows what that purpose might be, or if it is especially meaningful. We are all hungry for the meaning – for the purpose, for the feeling – that, actually, life has some kind of meaning. Humans are resourceful. We have infinite ways of finding meaning from infinite potential sources. We can find meaning in every scenario and in every event. We also know we want meaning in our lives and meaning helps us thrive. Have you ever asked yourself these questions: are you in the right place in life? Is the jigsaw puzzle of your life pieced together? We can spin over and over what we believe is the meaning and where it comes from, but there are so many ways to define meaning that it's impossible to narrow it down to just one or two best definitions. After all, meaning won't be the same for everyone. Feeling happy wasn't enough for me – I didn't want to simply exist on this beautiful earth, but to have a purpose. Having a purpose created true happiness for me.

When trouble hits you in your life, I think it's then you question its reason, its purpose and its meaning. I strongly believe that if you don't set your frequency to tune into a positive avenue, you will struggle to find life's meaning. Living in a jumbled mess of a broken mindset with no focus, no motivation and an incredibly low vibrational frequency delivers no direction to the meaning of life. It's commonly said that the route of most human unhappiness leads to feeling one's life has no meaning. It's fascinating to think deeply about what that means – the ideal life, the ideal meaning of life, why it has to have meaning, why we can't simply exist and walk the journey of life without putting pressure on ourselves to seek meaning. We can care about the wrong things for far too long and end up regretting wasting time and energy on something that hasn't given us the answers. When we experience tragic loss, specifically of a loved one, it's then we question everything past and present.

What you need to do is consider that, compared with the earth's existence, our time on this planet is extremely limited. This puts life into perspective and gives weight to finding your own meaning of life. The moment is now. Now is the time to think about your life. Don't waste any more time looking at your past. Look towards your future. What's gone is gone. We can't change what has passed, but we can turn the negatives into positives. Even if you lived to a hundred, there just aren't enough days in life. Live for the moment and don't dwell on the past. Our awareness of the present moment is, in some sense, already a memory. The past is a memory. It's a thought that's arriving in the present. The future is also a thought arriving in the present. So, what we have is this very moment, but we seem to forget to connect with the present moment. And we need to find fulfilment in it. Some people are quite happy with simply existing. As for me, I don't want to simply exist and die without a purpose and a reason. What matters is consciousness. Consciousness is everything. Experience of the world and our experience of the people we care about is a matter of consciousness.

This then begs the question how we can find fulfilment and how we can create lives that are truly worth living, given our lives will eventually come to an end. A life without meaning is a life of darkness. To wake in the morning with a purpose to your day gives fulfilment. You have the power within your mind to create your journey. Find your fulfilment. Create your meaning. You, the individual, have the world in your hands. Use the energy of the universe and make it work for you. Bring it into your energy, tune yourself into something positive and beautiful so that when you wake, you wake with meaning.

The question of the meaning of life is more interesting than the answer. I am no expert on life. I have made so many wrong mistakes, taken the wrong turn so many times, lived a life I never chose but one that was placed on me, possibly to test my strength. Wisdom cannot be gained in our younger years. We have to live experience to gain wisdom. And by sharing our wisdom with those younger than ourselves, we can hope to pass on a pinch of guidance. Life can deal incredibly tough cards. Some of us live to tell the tale. Some sadly don't. It's only through the trials and tribulations of life, the loves and the losses, you question the purpose of everything.

There is one saying that has stayed with me and that is: "Simply enjoy the passage of time." It's a simplistic outlook but is easy to understand. You can push yourself far too hard to find the meaning of life, and I believe the harder you push, the less you find. Use your experiences in life to guide you.

✱✱✱

In an interview, Elon Musk was asked what the meaning of life is. He proceeded to say he did question what it's all about when he was young and the conclusion he came to was: "Trying to understand the right questions to ask, and the more we can increase the scale and scope of human consciousness, the better we become at answering these questions." I had to really think about that and the more I did, the more it made sense. If we widen the scale of human consciousness, this then opens other doors, which increases our ability to understand more from life.

I realised I could no longer live the life I was living: if that was the meaning of life, then that journey was not for me. I fully admit I was not a nice person. I hurt a lot of people emotionally, I feared nothing, all I wanted was money and I didn't care how I obtained it. I didn't understand my existence. I believe life was preparing me for something new. My younger years were never meant to be an easy journey. I think I would've abused any goodness delivered to me early in life. I needed to have lived a life of failure to gain a life of happiness. This all sounds strange, I know, but it really does make incredible sense.

Someone once asked me what the meaning of life is. I replied by saying you've got to create your own meaning to suit your needs. It's what I've basically done with my life. I've used my past experiences to create my meaning of life in my later years. This may not work for everyone, but take your experiences, put them all in a pot, analyse them in depth and turn all the negative thoughts and failures into positives. Turning a negative into a positive is an incredible way of shining light into your life. If we learnt to take all the negative energy we use and turn it into positive thinking, how amazing would our strengths be? Using the adventure along the route of life is an amazing strength. Have faith and trust in the timings of your life.

✸✸✸

Gratitude

In some countries, children wake up with no food or water. Some children have to walk miles for a bucket of water which is polluted and could possibly kill them, and their mothers and fathers. In these starving countries, parents and children fail to grasp the thought that this will ever change for them. The food will continue to be minimal, and the water will continue to be polluted. Knowing families have lived with no hope for generations brings home the reality of life having no meaning. There is no hope. There is no change for the children, who will parent their own children in a world with no hope and no meaning. You might think everybody has a choice, but when you're faced with such a bleak future, there is no choice. For us in our cosy homes, yes, we may struggle to pay our bills and, yes, we may have to eat cheaply, but we have clean water and we do have food. And we have opportunities that can create change. We need to be thankful and grateful for what we have. We have to appreciate our existence.

Life isn't easy. It'll be tainted by betrayal and misguidance and broken promises, which might make you bitter, so you need to offset that and find your meaning. Take responsibility for yourself and take care of yourself physically and mentally. Find ways to improve yourself, with hope, and along that journey you will find your meaning.

The effect you have on your surroundings, the contribution you make to the rest of the world, that's what lifts life to a more meaningful existence. Making terminally ill children and their families smile and create memories – that's my contribution to life. It gives me great gratitude and gratitude is the greatest emotion. Practising gratitude has far-reaching effects, from improving mental health to boosting relationships. Living your life with gratitude helps you notice the little wins, like the bus showing up right on time, a stranger holding the door open for you, helping an elderly person across the road with their shopping, or even the sun shining through your window in the morning. Stringed together, these small moments create a web of well-being. Over time, this strengthens your ability to notice the good as well as the bad in others. Building your capacity for gratitude isn't difficult, it just takes practice. The more you bring your attention to what you feel grateful for, the more you will notice what you have to feel grateful for. Most of us know it's important to thank people who help us or silently acknowledge the things we are grateful for. Giving thanks can make you happier.

Gratitude turns what little you have into abundance. Gratitude is so much more than saying thank you; it can change your perspective of your world and all those around you. Gratitude is similar to appreciation. First comes the acknowledgement of goodness in our lives – we affirm that life is good and has elements that make it worth living. We should live with a deep sense of appreciation for the people who support us through difficult times, and for our health, our energy and our well-being. We should appreciate everything we have and maybe even the hardships we have had too.

Failure

What I'm trying to do here is show the chemistry behind everything that is the meaning of life. I'm still learning. I'm still gaining wisdom every day and taking daily steps to creating a better life and understanding my purpose. Why live life to simply exist? Life is like a film: it has a beginning and an end. Act out who you wish to be and your happy ending, so when you close your eyes on this life, you will have fulfilled every avenue. Go live your dream. Yes, you may fail from time to time, but from failure we grow. Without failure, we never learn. We all experience failure, but few know how to learn from it to be more successful.

It's natural to avoid things that could end in failure. Failure can be embarrassing and painful to experience. The problem is we read too much into failure and tie it to self-worth, self-esteem and self-acceptance. The expectation we failed to meet is often our own, one that we created in our heads. Most of us don't set out looking to fail at anything and we especially don't want to be labelled a failure, but maybe that's a mistake, because failure can be useful. We can learn from it, gain insights and do better next time. Failure gives us new information and teaches us something that gets us closer to our goals and understanding what life is truly about.

Happiness vs success

Don't confuse happiness with success. You could be quite happy eating a Chinese takeaway at home while watching TV, but that doesn't make you a success. Happiness is not a goal: it's a by-product of life. Success means attaining your vision of a good life. It means achieving specific goals that result in the future you have planned for yourself.

Those who have read *My Tormented Mind* will understand where I'm coming from here. I wasted decades with people who had no other purpose in my life than to destroy my journey. I misplaced my faith and trust in a lot of people, but I managed to turn that negative journey into a positive path ahead. I learnt the hard way, but I gained clarity. I discovered my purpose and I understand the meaning of my contribution to this life. My inner wealth is far richer than it's ever been. Yes, I live in a small council flat and I don't drive a flash car, but I have inner wealth. I have enough money to put food on my table and pay my bills. I am content. I enjoy seeing people smile. It lifts my vibrational frequency to a beautiful, happy place.

Of course, I have dreams, and maybe they will come true one day. I would love a little bungalow with a small garden, where my lovely cat, Poppy, could walk freely instead of on the concrete paths surrounding my flat. You have to have a dream in your heart. You have to find your purpose and reason to wake up every morning. Life can be beautiful. You need to reach out and embrace its energy. Live the life you wish to live and not the one dictated to you. Society can dictate your journey. Even your own family can dictate your journey. If you are happy with that journey, then embrace its path. Happiness is not a gift of life: you can create it. If you have breath in your body, legs that move freely, and a voice, then use these tools you have been blessed with and make it work for you – yes, you. Don't wait for the good life to fall into your lap with the blessing of all its fruits; you have to make it work yourself. Self-discipline is the key to success.

When I lost my beautiful friend, Jan, to cancer she said to me, while holding my hand, "I wish I could turn back the clock." Those very words are in my heart and soul and will never leave me. Nor the regret in my dear friend's eyes of not accomplishing her dreams. Even if they'd failed, she'd have attempted making them happen. The art of life is to live for your dreams. Anything can be achieved with self-belief. Nothing is impossible.

I hope this chapter gives you an incentive to create change in your life and find your meaning. How I see life now, in my fifties, is completely different to how I saw it in my twenties. We grow as individuals. Knowledge and wisdom have got me to where I am today, and I am going to embrace this journey ahead of me and learn to love life more and more each day.

Find your happy place in life and you will discover the meaning on your own terms. What I have shared with you, Reader, is my journey of discovery. You have to discover everything yourself, with the hope of finding your inner wealth. My prime purpose in life is to help others less fortunate and to create hope, love and smiles for everyone who enters my life each day.

"Every moment of your life is infinitely creative, and the universe is endlessly bountiful. Just put forth a clear enough request, and everything your heart desires must come to you."

— *MAHATMA GANDHI*

Chapter 6

The Law of Vibration: The Primary Law

Life is a process of self-discovery, and no experience is ever wasted. It only brings us closer to our evolution. It wasn't until I was lost that I began to discover myself and my purpose. It was then I embarked on the great adventure of my life and realised self-discovery was the greatest discovery. I began learning that if you have a sense of who you are, you will attract the right things in life. Amid my suffering, I found my truest self.

Throughout the rest of this book, I wish to share with you my awakening – the discovery of my own journey and my understanding of the law of vibration.

The law of vibration is the primary law. The law of attraction works as the secondary law, because vibration causes attraction. It is only when you invoke the law of vibration that the law of attraction can happen.

Everything that surrounds us is filled with energy. The entities of the universe are in constant vibration, seizing the greater powers all around us. Vibrational energy manifests an unseen force that drives all physical matter to convulse in different frequencies. Vibrational energy is a state of being; it is the environment; it is the energetic quality of a person, atmosphere, place, thought or act.

Even things that appear solid, like the chair you're sitting on, are made up of particles which are vibrating against one another, causing resistance and making it impossible to pass through. Your chair is pulsating with energy, as is every other solid item you can see or touch.

Consider colour. There are certain vibrational aspects of the colours of the rainbow that the human eye will connect to. Colour can change frequency. Violet vibrates at a higher frequency when it becomes ultraviolet.

You can even alter your own vibration by changing the way you think, feel or act. Within your mind is a field of energy, and the millions of thoughts you have every day create motion that sends out vibrational waves. This is where the law of attraction comes in. The law of attraction means "like attracts like". Whatever frequency you are vibrating at attracts a similar vibration. We live in what many people call an ocean of motion. Everything is built up of small molecules that are constantly vibrating. Your eyes can't see this, but it's happening.

✳✳✳

After losing my father in 1992, my life took a real tumble. My vibe was bad, which in turn meant I received that vibe back and always had negative people around me. This led the way for a very traumatic journey. My life was pure negativity. Only now, in my fifties, following my beautiful awakening, do I have a path of light ahead of me.

We may ask ourselves why we are not gifted with this discovery in our younger years. My answer to that is very simple: wisdom is the greatest teacher. Without it, we gain no knowledge. And without knowledge, there are no lessons learnt.

So, how do we find our happy frequency? With a mix of science and spirituality, I will describe my findings for you so you can see the potential value of using your vibrational frequency to live a healthy, happy life on every level.

At the beginning of this book, I touched on finding your focus and motivation as well as using meditation. The combination of these opened my third eye to there being something else out there that is energising and exceptionally beautiful. When you finally experience the alignment, life becomes one with your soul. I pay great attention to how I feel in my surroundings. Always be aware of how you feel at specific moments in time.

In writing this book, I wish to give you a spiritually energetic experience and share with you my wisdom and my discovery of a happier life. Your greatest wealth is your inner wealth – I truly believe that. You can have all the material things, but if you don't have inner wealth and happiness, your one and only life will be a dark place full of negativity. Writing has been an education for me. I've discovered beautiful avenues to experiment with and I hope to write further books to bring enlightenment to people's frequencies. However many years I have left on this beautiful planet, I want to live them happily, content in the thought that when I finally close my eyes on this life, I'll have given it my all, my best shot.

✳✳✳

One of the fundamental laws of the universe is the law of vibration, which says that almost everything moves, and nothing remains constant. Humans basically exist in a system of motion. When brain cells get activated, they set up a vibration within the body. To move our hands, we need to trigger brain cells to move them. Vibration is a mechanical process. The word 'vibration' originates from the Latin *vibrationem*, a shaking.

Everything vibrates through an external force, shaking or rapidly moving back and forth on a subatomic level. Everything carries vibrational energy. Even self-consciousness is a type of energy that vibrates at a very brisk pace.

✳✳✳

Vibrational patterns can calculate anything. During my research, I came across an experiment which took place many years ago. A mother rabbit was kept in a submarine while her baby was kept in a laboratory. To see how the mother rabbit would respond to her baby being killed, the mother rabbit was connected to equipment that tracks brain waves – her brain waves went off the scale the moment her baby was killed. Her calculated brain waves completely disappeared.

I am against animal testing, though while this experiment is painful to think about, it gives an insight into how I felt when I lost my mother. A mother carries her child for nine months, during which time mother and child make a spiritual connection that lasts into adulthood. When I witnessed my mother die in front of me, I immediately felt part of me die too.

I have always said that once the umbilical cord is cut, it is down to the child to survive life as we know it. However, a spiritual vibrational frequency will very much remain between the mother and the child. I will give you an example.

I was off work with the flu and suddenly felt the need to telephone my mother to see if she was OK. When I couldn't get a reply, I became worried and so I left home to go check on her. Call it gut instinct – that uncomfortable feeling that something isn't right. I arrived at her flat around midday and noticed the curtains were still closed and her lights were on in the living room. Straight away, I knew something was wrong. I panicked and ran towards the door. To my utter horror, I found her lying on the floor. My first thought was that she had fallen and died, but I soon realised she was still breathing. I managed to pick her up and sit her on the sofa. She had been lying there for approximately thirteen hours.

This is a prime example of gut feeling being telepathic connection. The feeling in my belly told me something was wrong. I then had the very same feeling when my mother passed away. As I watched her take her last breath, part of my soul died. Within two weeks of her passing, I too ended up in hospital, after attempting to take my own life. In hospital, I felt comforted – my mother's body was just corridors away in the mortuary. It was a strange but beautiful feeling, as if my mother was there with me. I don't believe there is nothing after this life, but the human body is a field of energy that continues to live on after death. We just travel to another world, which isn't separate from this one. I believe spirits move around us constantly, especially our loved ones, and I believe our energy lives on and we all meet again on a new level of energy.

The mother rabbit felt the loss of her child telepathically. Telepathy is something I strongly believe in. I can only describe it as a universal vibrational frequency. As the saying goes, "You have read my mind." This also might explain how some people, twins for example, can feel the emotions of someone they're close to. What this proves is that everything is linked: though we exist individually, we are all essential components of universal consciousness. People can interact with the whole of the universe.

✳✳✳

This law of vibration is part of the broader picture. The rule is to respond through superconsciousness: the ideas, feelings and emotions we send out.

The law of attraction is a major communicator in the vibrational pattern signature in which people send out their consciousness. Universal consciousness turns that vibrational pattern into reality by giving back what we put out there, whether positive or negative. The law itself doesn't judge right or wrong, but it is better to discover abundance, happiness and quality of life.

The law of attraction states like objects attract similar things. The universe represents thoughts and emotions as vibrations and reacts by giving space beyond one's thought process. Being in a positive state of mind causes our thoughts to vibrate at a higher frequency. Doubts decrease the frequency at which our thoughts vibrate and therefore the world responds moderately to them. Individuals who stay positive will stay within a strong vibrational mode when they are in a strong vibrational zone. Good things will always happen, along with positive vibes, therefore we need to vibrate with a positive mind. We need to control the vibration that stirs up the thought process, so people should remember to use the law of vibration positively and follow the law of attraction. These laws go hand in hand – they're not separate. The law of attraction can be used to direct individuals to the correct pattern of thought to obtain a deeper meaning of how it works with the law of vibration.

Combined, the laws can bring wealth, health, success and happiness. Thoughts, emotions and behaviours have their own vibrational rates, and these vibrations create resonance. Science shows that everything in the manifested universe consists of energy modules. Even solid objects have their own, sometimes deeper, frequency. Thinking is where everything starts. When the conscious mind thrives on the ideas of a certain quality, it then becomes deeply rooted in the subconscious mind and becomes a powerful sound with other similar vibrations.

Vibrations influence everything in the atmosphere. People and animals all resonate a vibrational frequency. Human sensations vibrate with energy. Positive emotions stand for positive situations, and negative emotions lead to negative conditions. Whether a solid, a liquid or a gas, everything in the universe is in motion. All objects move, vibrate and fly in circular patterns with their unique vibrational frequencies. Frequency is defined per unit of time; that is, the number of periodic oscillations, waves and vibrations. No two objects are completely alike in the universe as each has its vibrational design. This opens the door between substance and energy.

Vibrations are sent out into the world by feelings, emotions and desires. Every thought process or mental state has a matching vibrational rate and direction. The stronger the vibration, the longer the results. Optimists present stronger vibrational frequencies; pessimists present lower vibrational frequencies. Both frequencies can lift or lower the vibration of the planet. Vibrations affect your environment as well as the people around you. You will either draw in good or you will draw in bad, depending on what you are giving out to the universe.

Throughout my childhood and into my adulthood, I delivered a negative vibrational frequency and that in turn delivered me a negative journey. I only realised the severity of this through counselling. My journey was one I never chose. Those around me were programming my mind and my vibrational state into negative energy, which I then delivered into the universe and to everybody around me. Sending out thoughts of envy, disapproval and criticism, as well as hatred, will arouse others to this energy and return the same.

✳✳✳

Mobile phones and long periods of social media can interrupt your vibrational frequency and thought process. They hinder positive thinking and send out wrong human signals. We all have our unique sound and identity, and if we delved deep into the power of our minds, we would all benefit greatly. If we learnt to communicate with certain sounds, we would discover our true potential in life, as well as be able to communicate on a much more productive level.

Every human being has the option to choose the energy that will establish inner peace. Start by selecting positive choices and activities to balance your body and your behaviours. The food you eat will affect your mind. If you rely on drugs and alcohol to feel good, your mental journey especially will be non-productive. You need to take care of your mind by collecting healthy thoughts and finding that spiritual energy and growth for a blessed journey. Negative thoughts will prevent you from obtaining the quality of life you deserve. When you choose the positive route, you can step with calculated progress to reach your spiritual goals.

Regular failures and setbacks can make it seem like things are never going to progress. When we feel like this, the mind generates vibrational frequencies based on those feelings. To solve our problems, we must learn to position our hearts, minds and thoughts to a higher frequency since higher frequencies create greater awareness. We can then find the answers that can only be found in the higher realm of life. The art of keeping your vibrational state high is not letting negative influences affect your vibrational energy. Living in a world surrounded by negativity, that's easier said than done. However, we must learn to send out the right signals to receive the right signals in return, and, if we do, maybe our influence will lift the vibrational state of those who are on negative paths. But remember this could drain your energy if left for too long. If enough of us pursued and learnt to live by the law of vibration – if we learnt to tune ourselves into the universe and work as one – we could make this beautiful world a better place, a more positive place.

One way I have found to not disrupt my happiness is to not get too concerned with other people's problems. I became too involved in negative people and it drained my resources, which in turn disrupted any positive path I was on. I'm talking about people who generally have no interest in pursuing a happy life, those who drink heavily and take drugs. Being around people like that, who weren't living a real life, was extremely damaging to my mindset. For me to continue the journey I am now on, which I have no intention on leaving, I've had to remove certain people from my life. As I approach fifty-three, I live to love and help those less fortunate. I keep away from those who don't want to better their lives. It sounds harsh, but I have limited precious time on this earth, so I don't intend to waste it. 'Do not suffer fools gladly' is something I ignored for far too long.

Set targets for problem solving and use the law of vibration to embrace every moment, every thought, every feeling, every emotion, every action. I will deliver a permanent level for as long as I can each and every day and I hope this will help everyone in my circle. We all need to get into a positive frame of mind. That is what it takes to make this world a better place. You need to get yourself in line before you can progress to a successful state of mind.

The law of vibration relates to everything being a source of energy, and that energy is the making of the entire universe. When you've mastered that, the law of vibration will deliver whatever you dream. The law of vibration can improve your life, and everything in it, even your relationships. The law of vibration and the law of attraction must be aligned through both the conscious and the subconscious mind. The law of vibration tells us a reaction occurs for any action. In other words, for every one of us, there is an impact as well as a trigger. It is possible to get something you want simply by dreaming about it; however, you need to modify your subconscious thoughts for this to work. If the subconscious mind doesn't need the thing you want, you simply won't have it. Concentrate on conditioning your subconscious mind in such a way it vibrates in sync with the universe's vibrations, simply by thinking about it. I should make it clear it's the mind not the brain that's at work.

The mind uses the brain to carry out specific tasks, and the conscious mind analyses and processes feedback from our senses.

To get what you want from life, the laws of vibration and attraction need to be implemented simultaneously. The conscious mind will acknowledge the feedback and then relay it to the subconscious mind. The subconscious mind needs to be capable of vibrating in line with the universe. If you don't make certain lifestyle adjustments, you won't reach this state. Only ever seek positive vibrations to find your happy frequency. There is a force people use to exert this influence, which is said to affect anything from people's minds to physical objects. This mysterious force has been labelled as witchcraft. Witches use certain ingredients in their spells to change vibrational frequencies to obtain certain goals. I do not recommend trying this.

We can interpret a lot about vibrations from the Bible. Firstly, we can understand that God has created all things in such a way that they give off vibrations, and the more we turn to God and the more we focus on positivity, the better those vibrations get. The law of attraction is two entities attracting or repelling based on their frequencies.

Jesus is often depicted with a glowing heart in the centre of his body. This is the solar plexus, the perfect intersection of nerves and arteries, the soul's abode. The human mind is an important part of vibration, but it is the heart that holds the strength. People make the mistake of only using their mind to construct their reality, but until they have belief in their hearts, they'll only experience minimal success. The heart is what keeps the body alive. The energy from this centre point is incredibly powerful. The heart has around 40,000 neurons that are very similar to the brain's neurons. I stumbled across some interesting research which backs up the importance of listening to your heart. The heart generates emotion and works with frequency to generate an energy like sound waves, which is distributed into the world. Our thoughts can travel far and wide and translate to similar energies and frequencies and emerge bigger in the process.

Every second of every day of every month, someone sends a vibration out into the world. It might be a good vibration. It might be a bad one. I would love to share with you how giving out positivity can give you a better life. You can make your dreams a reality. The law of vibration says we belong to something far greater than we can imagine. When you know this, you can work in line with universal consciousness, which we are all linked to. All paths lead to the same end, and all things are derived from the same source. Just a simple smile or frown you give in passing affects the energy people spread. I like to send out energy that transmits peace and love on every level. Peace, love and understanding.

Remember this change happens within. Life will only reflect what you give it, just like a mirror will. The mirror has no choice but to smile back at you. Physical reality is just a mirror. The true measure of change is reaching the state you want, regardless of what's going on around you. Everything is energy: embrace it. When you match the frequency of the reality you want, you cannot help but reach that reality.

"My soul is the mirror of the universe, and my body is its frame."

— *VOLTAIRE*

Chapter 7

The Sun of God

The beautiful radiant sun. That big bright glow in the sky that makes us all feel so much happier. Its pure brightness is a smile maker and lifts our spirits to another level.

During my low days throughout the summer of 2022, I would drive to my sanctuary at Aylesford Priory to absorb the sun's radiance and pray. My newfound faith in the power of the universe gave light into the power of the sun. During my counselling I walked that lost child who had been locked away in my adult soul for decades into a beautiful bright light. It was as if the sun was inviting my child soul and my adult soul to reunite in God's kingdom of light. From that moment on, the sun became my god. Yes, my god. I find comfort in its energy and it lifts me to a higher vibrational state.

I don't see God as a physical image but as energy. The creator of all is energy and everything is energy. Energy has been called 'God' from as far back as the 6th century, in the Codex Argenteus (which can be literally translated as the 'Silver Book'). The Codex Argenteus contains part of a 4th century translation of the Christian Bible into the Gothic language.

The Bible records people witnessing God and describing him as a brilliant light and as a fire because of his burning passion. These encounters with God took place over about 1,500 years, from Moses to John the Apostle to Ezekiel, Daniel and Isaiah. Their descriptions are quite similar. In John 4:24, God is a spirit and so his appearance is not like anything we can describe.

God's first act as creator was to call light into each being and separate it from the darkness. God said "Let there be light" and there was light, and God divided the light from the darkness. God is light and he is surrounded by light that speaks of his beauty, holiness and purity. James describes God as the father of light because God is pure and constant in his goodness and purity (James 1:17). God wants you to live in his light and he relates to us in the manifestation of his light. The greatest blessing is to have the light from God's face shine on you. This is part of the blessing that Aaron the priest would pray over the people of Israel, in the Old Testament.

In the age to come, we will live in the light of God (Revelations 4:3) and add deep red – carnelian. In the Bible, God's glory was manifested as red fire, cloud, lightning and thunder. Moses was tending the flock of his father-in-law, Jethro, the priest of Midian. Moses led the flock to Mount Horeb, where he witnessed the angel of the lord appear in his glory in the burning bush (Exodus 3:2,6). Moses learnt that God is holy, separate.

Isaiah saw the seraphim, the burning ones, around the throne of God (Isaiah 6:2). Daniel saw the throne of God as a flame (Daniel 7:9). Other descriptions depict his throne surrounded by a rainbow. God appeared to those tempted by his mercy; the rainbow speaks of God's mercy, patience and faithfulness. This is great news because otherwise no one would be in his kingdom.

One thing to note is that the fullness of God's glory would be too much for us to see in this life. "You cannot see my face, nor no one may see me and live." (Exodus 33:20). You can't stare directly at the sun without damaging your eyes – and the sun is millions of miles away. We are not just talking about God as a physical intensity but one who is perfect and holy. I'm far from an expert on the Bible; however, what research I have done tells me there is no real image of God other than as a bright light from the sky – in visions of rainbows, lightning and thunder. I see God as a pure energy and nothing else.

When I pray, I pray to an energy. When I wake in the morning, I hold out my hands and take three deep breaths in, hold and exhale. I then give my affirmations for the day. Even if it is cloudy and there is no sun, I know I am expressing my affirmation to the universe and sending it my vibrational frequency. This works for me. Everybody has their own way of praying depending on their practices and religion. However you find peace, stay with what you believe. Whether you pray to a tree, the soil or the sea, if you find comfort in it, you must carry on doing what you do. We all find comfort differently.

The way I look at things is that if nobody has a true description of God, I can form my own image of him. I can feel his presence, I can feel his energy, I can see the light described in the Bible and in other religious work. When I pray, I want to pray to something I can see. I see the visible energy of God.

✳✳✳

Sun worshipping has been practised for a great many years, though relatively few cultures – Egyptian, Indo-European and Mesoamerican – developed solar religions. These groups had in common a well-developed urban civilisation with a strong ideology of sacred kingship. They had the imagery of the sun as ruler of both the upper and the lower worlds. In Ancient Egypt, the sun god was the dominant figure among the high gods and he retained this position from early in the civilisation's history. The sun god occupied a central position in both the Sumerian and Akkadian civilisations. The sun was one of the most popular deities, but the Indo-European people believed it to be a symbol of divine power.

Sun worship gained importance in Roman times and ultimately led to solar monotheism. Nearly all the gods of that period possessed solar qualities and both Christ and the god Mithra acquired the traits of the solar deities.

In the pre-Columbian civilisations of Mexico and Peru, sun worship occupied an important place in myth and ritual, and human sacrifice was demanded by the sun gods. The ruler in Peru was an incarnation of the Inca sun god Inti.

The sun goddess Amaterasu played an important role in ancient Japanese mythology and was considered the supreme ruler of the world. This was the tutelary deity of the imperial clan, and to this day the sun symbol represents the state of Japan.

The high god, or the sky god, is a supreme deity found among non-literate peoples of North and South America, Africa, northern Asia and Australia. Native Americans and Central and South Africans believe thunder to be the voice of the high god.

In Siberia, the sun and the moon are considered the high god's eyes. The sacredness of the moon is linked to the basic rhythms of life and the universe, and moon worship has engineered rich symbolism and mythology.

My two years of research into what the sun, the universe and its energy symbolise in religion, and their benefits to the soul, has been enlightening. I cannot express enough my inner transformation. This new light within me has energised my soul to a level of pure strength. I am no longer looking for a life of unforeseen work with no meaning. I wish to wake in the morning with a true purpose in life. Material possessions mean nothing to me. If you are looking for change, then don't waste any more time. I have had a spiritual awakening, like a butterfly emerging from its cocoon. Once you transform to a higher level of consciousness, it's only then you realise the power you have. My prayer is delivered with an energy which gives me a bulletproof sense of inner peace, no matter the circumstances in my life. I feel at one with everyone and everything. The most important emotion is love and to love unconditionally is the path of peace for all living beings. To find your true self is your true path. I now have a deep healing of mind, body and spirit. And a permanent higher shift in consciousness and the capacity to fundamentally change my direction in life.

There is no real secret to any of this; however, you need to take time for yourself to have this awakening and use an energy that is visible. And that visible energy is the sun. The sun is the powerhouse of the solar system. It's been generating energy for 4.5 billion years, and it will continue to burn for another 5 billion. Energy radiates from the centre of our solar system in the form of light, heat, gamma rays and X-rays, and magnetic fields. Every day the sun shines, it drives chemical and physical changes across the planet. Some of the energy that comes from the sun is easy to see and feel; other energy isn't always obvious, and you need tools to detect and observe it. The heat, light and radiation from the sun are forms of electromagnetic radiation. Unlike forms of energy that need to move through matter (like sound), electromagnetic radiation can travel through the vacuum of space, without other atoms, molecules or particles to carry it. These waves of energy are part of the electromagnetic spectrum that encompasses everything from long radio waves to two very short gamma rays. Visible light and invisible light such as infrared radiation and ultraviolet radiation (UV) are all part of the electromagnetic spectrum.

White light is a combination of all the colours. When scientists view distant stars, they use spectroscopy to split the light and analyse the colours, just how white light shining through a crystal or prism breaks apart the light into different colours.

✳✳✳

I am fascinated by the sun. No matter what is thrown at me during my day, the sun will make me smile. If you take a moment to find peace and feel the sun's energy on your face, you'll immediately feel comforted. The sun can help us all. When the light from above enters your every cell, it powers your body more than any other energy. It's an unseen energy that shakes within you, shifting and moving you and changing who you are. Embrace the light and your body will react in profound ways. The more connected to the sun you are, the better your energy will vibrate. During my awakening I found I required the sun a lot more. I've always loved the sunshine but now I see it in an entirely different way. The more I feel the sun, the more I feel connected to everything around me. If you learn to embrace and understand its connection, if you learn to look deeper into your spiritual side and connect with an unseen energy, you will find a heightened sense of what I call 'awakening'. There is something which connects the sun to the deepest part of our souls. For me, it's not written in a scripture, it's not delivered to me in words. The only way I can describe it is information that comes to me in a vibrational frequency, to be absorbed.

Sit in a sunny place to absorb the sun and ask yourself how you feel. Then on a rainy, cold, miserable day, ask yourself how you feel again. It's a very simple experiment which delivers a very simple answer. Does the sun make you feel better? Just spending a few minutes outside gives your body energy and makes you feel amazing. Every cell in your body will resonate with the sun's energy. Try and manage your day with the rhythms of the sun. You will feel energised, and your day will have much more structure to it. Make sure you have a healthy breakfast and drink lots of water. You can even charge water by leaving a glass in the sunlight, to give it an extra boost of energy. The sun's energy is normally extremely high around noon. I love this ritual. I go outside and I connect with the sun around noon, when it's at its highest point. I'm only talking minutes. I visualise a beautiful glowing light coming down and embracing my body. Feel it connecting with your heart and your soul, energising your internal organs. Give yourself a smile, smile to the sun, let it know how happy you are, give yourself gratitude for who you are.

The sun is the life-giving force. There is always the beautiful magical dance between the earth and the sun and the moon. The sun is essential for energy and vitality. My most favourite time to embrace the sun's energy is first thing in the morning. During the summer months it's the best time for prayer as it's not so hot. Seeing the sun activates my pineal glands, which immediately triggers my body's natural rhythms. Find a time suitable for you to comfortably sit in the sun and experience its energy. I love sunrise and sunset. How incredibly beautiful it is for the human eye to witness this.

Try to make an emotional connection with the earth. Walk barefoot. Use the source of life, the source of your body and then connect with the sun, the life force – the *prana*, the life-giving energy. When you make this link, you will heal.

I hope this chapter has given you food for thought. I wanted to share with you how beneficial the sun's energy is. Everything comes down to the same aspect of the sun, and that is energy. I pray to the sun and when I do, I let the energy flow to the universe with an intent to resonate and send a reply in its own way. The unseen language, I call it. It returns me a magical gift, and that's happiness. My happiness then spreads to those around me and that can only be a good thing in today's world. Spread that happiness, even down to a simple smile – you never know, it could brighten someone's day. My newfound vibrational frequency delivers beautiful gifts. Learn to use its mysterious ways and let the universe guide you to a happier place.

"Keep your face to the sun and you will never see the shadows."

— *HELEN KELLER*

Chapter 8

Awakening of Nature

Nature has the ability to be imbued with spiritual power. Forests and mountains invoke the divine and enlightenment. I regularly visit Aylesford Priory, my beautiful sanctuary, where I sit beside a beautiful lake and listen to the sound of the water brushing against the sides. I never really gave nature much thought before my awakening; life strolled from one day into the next. There was no embracing nature because I hadn't grasped how beneficial it was, not only to my soul but to my health in general.

I wasn't looking for an awakening, but it found me. I've mentioned how I meditate on Shirley B's memorial bench. During one particular meditation, I tuned into a beautiful birdsong. I gently opened my eyes to see a red robin on a branch directly in front of me. As the little robin played its tune, I realised it had made me smile. My troubles and my anxiety didn't feel so close by. I then took notice of two other birds singing in tune with my energy. This amazing experiencc is something I will never forget. When the robin flew away, I gave myself gratitude. You may be asking why I would thank myself for this experience. The reason is if I hadn't taken the time for myself that day, I would not have discovered the spiritual beauty of nature right before my eyes.

I learned something valuable that day: my energy connection with nature. Nature gave me something which lifted my soul and made me smile. Day-to-day life can be so overwhelming. The modern world is driven by technology – mobile phones, social media, computers – which takes us away from connecting with nature, even if not intentionally. We need to reconnect with nature to enjoy a more blessed existence. This beautiful planet is a field of amazing vibrational energy. We exist within nature, therefore it's normal to feel a connection or a pull towards it.

Life is full of obligations and responsibilities. We worry far too much about things that haven't even happened. Life can be draining at times and there isn't always an opening to release the stress. I'm talking on every level – losing a loved one, battling drug and alcohol abuse, relationship problems, the pressure of work, survival. The feeling of simply existing, with no light at the end of the tunnel. By reconnecting with nature, you can become more grounded in your existence. Life can be overwhelming, but nature helps us remember beauty and calm. My own discovery brought me peace, through learning how to focus and giving myself time to locate the inner wealth I had so strived to find. Once I found my inner peace, other doors opened, shining light into my energy. Combining my connection with the earth and the universe's vibrational energy gave me an insight into other areas I never would have explored. You've got to find yourself before you can grow. It's only then the universe will offer you its beauty, but it's there for the taking. You just need to take the time to slow down. Your fears and troubles will ease, you simply need to set your vibrational frequency with the earth. Everything around you will change. The energy of the universe will work in tune with you, just like the tuning forks.

So how can you begin to establish a spiritual connection with nature? Start going for long walks in the countryside or by the sea. You could find a park or trail to walk down, depending on where you live and on your needs. In my experience, walking around your local streets or town centre won't give you the peace that walking in the countryside or your local park will. Negative interference from traffic, sirens, people shouting won't benefit your mind, heart and soul.

Be mindful: take in trees and birdsong. There is a tree at Aylesford Priory that's well over a hundred years old. Every time I walk into the rosary garden, I place my hand upon that tree to embrace its deep-rooted energy. I think of all the things it has witnessed along its journey, yet survived to tell the tale. In this crazy, busy world we live in, it reminds me of my place and priorities and is a powerful and vital tonic.

Notice the flowers, animals, insects. You'll feel more grounded and connected if you take the time to be mindful. Start by noticing the little connections in nature. All animals play a role in maintaining the ecosystem and there is a powerful sense of togetherness in that. Don't separate yourself from nature; think about your role in the ecosystem too. We are one of many creatures on this planet, but it's easy to lose sight of that. Instead of seeing ourselves as part of the earth, we often see ourselves as the earth's resources and this causes problems for both us and the planet. When you focus on your connection to the earth, you have a much stronger sense of your role on this planet.

The connection between humans and pets is truly amazing. After witnessing two tragic deaths, which left me traumatised, I discovered the love I had for my mother's cat, which I had bought her a year before she passed away. She had had a cat called Tigger for nineteen years prior. Tigger was her soulmate. Throughout the darkest days of my life, in my mother's flat with nothing but silence and despair, I began to gain comfort from my mother's new cat, Poppy. This bundle of fluff gives me unconditional love. To this day, she sits beside me and purrs. It's absolutely beautiful. Poppy lifts my spirits and because there are no conditions, it makes her energy an energy of pure love.

The best thing you can do for yourself and for others is to keep an open mind to the benefits of nature. Understand that the world is full of new perspectives. As we grow up, we establish opinions about certain things, but by keeping an open mind you can welcome others' opinions and accept them as you do your own. One of the most powerful ways to embrace positive vibrational energy is to understand your inherited connection to nature as well as to humans. We all exist on this planet together and you can open yourself to positive vibrational frequency simply by connecting with nature.

I have found that many people are now searching for the sense of belonging to something bigger than themselves. Maybe this has happened to you. Maybe you've gone for a walk one day and beams of sunlight have warmed your skin and all of a sudden you've felt you are a living thing, part of an ecosystem. Sometimes I imagine I'm on a mountain peak, in awe of the view below. I picture myself enduring physical and mental challenges to shift my perspective and see these transformations and their benefits.

✳✳✳

Ancient wisdom describes human beings as having five layers of experience: the environment, the physical body, the mind, intuition, and our self or spirit. How we connect with the environment is our first level of pure experience, and one of the most important. If our environment is clean and positive, it has a positive impact on the other layers of our existence. As a result, they come into balance, and we experience a greater sense of peace and connection within ourselves and with others around us. An intimate relationship with the environment is built into the human psyche. Nature – mountains, rivers, trees – and the sun and the moon have always been honoured in ancient cultures. When we start moving away from our connection to nature and ourselves, we begin polluting and destroying the environment. We need to revive these attitudes that foster our connection with nature.

Today, we live in a world of greed, where people want to achieve quick results to make quick profits. Their actions disrupt the ecological balance and not only pollute the physical environment, but themselves and those around them. These negative energies then get compounded. Damage to the environment takes a long time to repair. We need to attend to the human psyche, which is the root cause of both physical and emotional pollution.

✳✳✳

I wish to share some pointers to help you discover a way to connect with nature, look deeply within yourself and give gratitude for who you are. Sometimes we become the person we never chose to be. My family never really showed me love and so I lost connection to the emotional feeling of being loved. I never truly understood love, yet I knew how to give affection to deliver love. My childhood trauma led to a destructive adulthood, which then delivered negative energy throughout my life. Nature, though, gave me an element of unconditional love. The more love I gave to nature, the more it loved me in return.

It's all too easy to lose sense of who you are. I never became the person, friend or son I dreamt of being. None of us live to perfection. We all have our faults and we have to come to terms with our pasts. Since we cannot change what has passed, we need to embrace tomorrow as an energy that will deliver us a brighter future.

I love walking, especially through fields of long grass. I want to *feel* the grass, the earth, the sky, the sun, the streams and lakes. I don't just want to gaze at them, I want to *feel part of* them. I want to feel nature's mood – its peace and its rage – and its infinite night-time beauty. Imagine a spirit in the dark clouds rolling into life, giving water to the earth. Imagine the spirit of the sun giving warmth and light to us all. Notice how the spirit of the sky is filled with you. You are surrounded by stars, planets, animals and plants, which are all part of the greater whole.

Have you ever been out for a jog or a drive and spotted a beautiful field or tree and it's been a revelation? Like a deep peace is settling into you? Maybe you've been at the seaside and felt an energy and then suddenly everything feels right in the world. Nature is not just a collection of trees and rocks and animals and plants, but a presence unto itself, and you as a human are part of it. Call it God if you like. Again, I refer to God as an energy. I've come to think of these moments of clarity, connection and peace as accidental encounters with nature. You weren't necessarily seeking a profound experience, but it happened, as it did with me that beautiful summer's day while meditating on that bench. Many of us never go further than living and surviving. Many of us never experience the connection between our mother earth and the universe and the beauty of nature within. These accidental encounters with nature are just the beginning. They are the doorway, the invitation to discover your own nature and to live your life with nature. I had become a ghost hovering around the edges of my own life. Eventually, I realised this hole from losing my mother and little Lyrah could never be filled. Like a flower turning towards the sun, I felt my way towards nature.

What I discovered is that it is possible to shift from an accidental spiritual relationship with nature to an intentional one. I began to spend time in nature, consciously connecting with it. Nature became my spiritual path to energising my vibrational frequency. I began to learn I was never truly alone despite my family being gone or having no interest in my well-being. Nature gave me not only a friend but a beautiful existence I never knew existed. The reason I meditate is it allows me to walk through the doors of nature. Our lives are busy and our minds even busier. Meditating closed all those doors, which then allowed me to walk into pastures new. You need to listen and communicate with nature. I understand this doesn't come naturally, which is why I use meditation to connect me to it. However, you can find happiness and peace simply by walking through a field, as I do when I walk through the rosary garden at Aylesford Priory. Even without meditation, the feeling that brings is truly beneficial to your inner wealth.

Nature really can guide us. We can ask ourselves what this interaction means. For me, it means peace and happiness. When I look back over my childhood, specifically on memories I don't feel comfortable with, I realise they were transformative moments. This is all spiritual development, which awakens your soul to the path you truly wish to be on. I would never have discovered this if it wasn't for my counselling sessions with Julie. I sincerely believe I would not be alive today if it wasn't for my awakening. I was suicidal. I thought of suicide every minute of every second of every day.

My awakening shows me a beauty I never took notice of. I now use my eyes and ears and am constantly listening to nature and looking for those beautiful birds singing in the trees and the squirrels in the cemetery where I visit my mother and father. The doves and pigeons I feed daily give me such a strength of connection with the earth and the universe. This all helps me make better choices. It calms my heart. The more I learn, the more I trust nature. Step outside and take a look at your community around you – the fox running the streets at night, the tiny birds sitting on your washing line. Say good morning to the sparrow sitting on your fence. See what you receive.

I believe humans are losing their spiritual connection with one another, which is sadly making them lose their connection with nature. Some of my findings explored the hypothesis that humans have become alienated from nature. How can we establish this important connection with nature? Learn by embracing the natural beauty around you – it delivers peace and serenity and connects us to something larger than ourselves. Humans were once so intimately connected to nature their basic needs derived directly from it. Nowadays, the closest the majority of the human race get to nature is watching a nature programme on the television set. Not only have we lost our connection to nature from the essence of survival, we have become alienated from the spiritual essence of that connection.

✳✳✳

This has been a deeply empowering time for me. I remember walking to the Royal Navy Memorial on the Gillingham lines field and realising my footprints were the only footprints behind me. There and then, I realised the power of solitude and what it really means. Solitude often has sad connotations, but my solitude was a choice. As a child, I'd spend hours on my own. I felt comfortable on my own; I felt safe. I had a pet dog called Blackie from the age of five to eighteen. That beautiful little dog loved me unconditionally, which, to this day, warms my heart. I have spent most of my life alone, so, for me, being alone has no undertones. For me, it's a powerful state of choice and calm. The footprints I took notice of were an indication of how my life has been for almost fifty-three years. But I am no longer alone because, now, nature is my friend, my partner, my soulmate. Nature restored my faith in love. The more I love nature, the more it makes me smile. I no longer feel deeply unhappy and I'm not lonely. I'm at one with the universe and I'm no longer alone.

The more I embrace nature, the more I learn to take notice of it – like how sunlight on my face boosts my physical and spiritual well-being. I sometimes drive to a place called Sheerness, in Kent, where you can park your car almost on the beach. I have always loved the sea. I love parking up on the shore, watching the waves brush up and down. It feels in harmony with my soul. The energy I get from watching the tides come and go is so uplifting. You can find solitude on any given day, under a tree in the street, on a bench in the park, even in a quiet place in a coffee shop. You can find your place of solitude. My connection is specifically with nature. Nature isn't just something you glimpse when you're out in the countryside; it's around us everywhere; it's our roots and wings. Connecting is what's required. I believe it's what we all subconsciously crave.

I have learned to take notice of the scent of nature, the smell of flowers during the summer months. Once all your senses are activated, you'll feel acutely alive. Furthermore, engaging our senses brings us in touch with the here and now and makes resting our attention on the present moment seem effortless. Natural places have an infinite reservoir of discoveries, supplying us with adventures and thrills and smiles. They're therapeutic. I even realised how therapeutic it is listening to rain hit the window.

Embracing nature is embracing a higher power as a relationship. It has taken my connection to another level. I find myself part of a beautiful living earth and universe, where everything is entwined as one energy. Nature is the link between human and universal energy. Embrace nature and you will find the link to a vibrational frequency which opens areas of your soul you would never otherwise look into.

Sadly, human beings have become an indoor species. Many properties are built with concrete surroundings with nothing other than the occasional tree and very little natural wildlife. But this shouldn't stop you from connecting with nature. Simply planting a seed in a plant pot at home and watching it grow is a connection with nature. I don't believe watching nature programmes on the television connects you with nature spiritually. You need to feel and smell and absorb its reality. If you don't have your own transport to get to a local park, there is always the bus or the train. We all have options: it's a case of getting off your armchair and going to find it. We have become incredibly lazy, working, returning to the sofa and then going to bed. This is such a common routine and a sad disconnection between humankind and nature. Having the occasional holiday does not bring about a connection with nature, because holidays are normally a break from work. You can make a conscious decision to spend more time in nature and embrace the host of benefits to your body, mind and spirit. Nature can play a profound role in healing your body and mind while unifying your true identity and spiritual being. Also known as eco therapy or green therapy, spending time in nature cultivates a state of holistic balance and growth through nourishing interaction with the earth.

I hope this chapter has made you think about how you can lift your energy just by taking a moment to listen to nature. It costs you nothing but your time. From being suicidal to having a peaceful mind, connecting with the earth and the universe through nature will take your vibrational frequency to enlightenment.

Enjoy the experience – you won't regret it.

"The goal of life is to make your heartbeat match the beat of the universe, to match your nature with nature."

— *JOSEPH CAMPBELL*

Chapter 9

Healing and Well-Being

Healing energy, the universe and you. After losing my mother and little Lyrah, I had to find ways to heal. I managed to gain focus and found a solid base of strength. I meditated and I began to understand the connection between us as humans and the energy of the universe. I began to understand the meaning of life. One thing I certainly discovered is the older I'm getting, the more I'm leaving behind. I had to come to terms with my trauma as my general health was declining. I began to research healing and well-being specifically in connection to the universe and its positive energy. Healing is no great mystery. Everyone has healing energy and the ability to heal themselves and others. Everything in the universe is energy, from stars to stones and even specks of dust. The flow of energy in the body is directly affected by our awareness, thoughts and feelings. Problems arise when there is an interruption to the flow of energy and too much accumulates in a particular place. This excess gives rise to imbalance, bodily congestion and disease. It is difficult to feel cheerful every waking moment, but the more positive you are, the healthier and happier you are likely to be.

Healing deals with excess energy. When we are ill or not feeling ourselves, we might be lacking in energy. We may feel lethargic or very tired. Whatever the symptoms, there is inevitably a blockage somewhere in our system. Feeling low, depressed and anxious can seriously affect our internal organs – and question our long-term health. When too much energy has accumulated, it does not stay still; by its very nature, energy is always moving. It will form unwanted complex patterns which can cause health problems. Since the body is energy, the essence of healing is to create the right conditions for the excess to return to the environment – to the universe – and restore balance.

There was very little awareness of well-being when I was growing up in the seventies. I loved affection, though I never received it in any way, shape or form. Affection can lift your vibrational frequency and bring a smile. I love to smile. If we all learned to smile more often, what a world this would be. The effect smiling has on others can be truly beneficial. A simple hug and a smile open the body's energy channels and release all those blockages. Learn to smile at yourself. Breathe in, smile to your body, breathe out and let your smile extend beyond your body. Try it for a minute or two. It is so simple but it is extremely effective at making us more receptive to healing energy.

During the first year and a half after losing my mother, my diet and general health were in serious question. I was drinking a lot, which I had never done before, and depression had a hold of me. This put me in hospital with a suspected heart attack. I had no fight left in me. Every speck of energy was gone. I was en route to pure destruction. My counselling with Julie helped me regain my mental energy, and I began to eat sensibly, which increased my physical energy. I have always been involved in the fitness industry and I've done weight training for thirty-five years. I understand the importance of good nutrition, but my body and mind were in such a dark place. Once I returned to a clean diet, my vibrational frequency lifted and my energy increased from week to week.

I began to research the importance of nutrition, with a view to lifting my energy levels further. I discovered that you can be gluten-free, eat a low-calorie diet, be vegetarian, eat organic-only produce, follow a ketogenic diet, do intermittent fasting with a little macrobiotic on the side, drink herbal tea and take every possible vitamin, protein shake, health supplement on the market and train every day on the stepper, on the treadmill, with weights – you can have all that in play, strategically planned, but if you don't take care of your responses to everyone and everything in your life, those negative signals you are sending to your cells will promote danger. Your cells will take those negative signals and damage your internal organs. You could end up seriously ill if your body isn't able to rest and restore. Your body will fail to digest, which will create an emergency in your body. How can you digest if your body's in fear there's going to be danger? If your mind is constantly afraid of what tomorrow might bring – a worrying business meeting, whether you can pay your electricity bill – the day-to-day grind will pull on your immune system. Without positive energy, your body will stay in that maladaptive state and the imbalance will become the new balance. Your body will now be heading towards disorder, disease. Take my situation for example. When I let my trauma overtake my health, my state of mind was poor. As I've said, you could have the 'best' diet in the world and put in all the effort at the gym, but if your mind is in constant fear, your nervous system will be at risk. And that could lead to long-term health problems. I've known fitness fanatics who were afraid of tomorrow.

We live in a stressful society, where everything is on demand. Learn to schedule in time for joy in a way that you would an appointment. Treat yourself, create a smile for yourself, give yourself gratitude, give yourself time for you. Discover the real you. No matter how perfect your fitness regime and your diet, if you are constantly stressed, then all the work you're putting in will eventually result in a negative outcome. Learn to be kind to your soul. Embrace the energy of the universe: it's free and it's there for the taking, so use it. Don't wait for joy and happiness to find you: make it work for yourself. Live a healthier life by taking time for yourself and removing the negative energy from the stress your mind is manufacturing. Create a new version of you. The universe is always working for you, always looking out for you. Trust me, it's there.

My discovery is your discovery. Thoughts are the electrical charge to the quantum field, and feelings produce a magnetic charge to the quantum field. The way you think and the way you feel broadcast electromagnetic energy which influences every single atom in your life. Thoughts send the signals out to the universe, which in turn draws the experience back to you. So, if anger, resentment and frustration are holding the intention of your future, that's mind and body in opposition – there's no vibrational match between anything in your future. Have you ever asked yourself why you haven't been successful in everything you do?

I lived a very negative existence from the moment I was born. For fifty-two years, I was angry and resentful and this portrayed the wrong image of me to my family. Being sexually abused at the age of seven, and bullied by the person responsible, led to me almost taking my life. But counselling opened my third eye to a fresh and beautiful world. All the energy I'd placed into my negative journey, I put into turning my life around. I never thought I could write a book and here I am writing my second book on the experiences of my life. Don't give anyone the power to bring back the old version of you. To heal, I have had to deal with my trauma and finally lay it to rest. I was not going to let the people responsible dictate my future. Don't let anyone trigger an unhealed version of you. I am going to prove I am so much better than that. I can feel life changing for me – I can see beautiful lights in my horizon.

You can begin to make changes to the way you think. Here is a test. Look into the mirror, deep into your eyes, and say "I love you". Gratitude can work miracles. As a child, I struggled with expressing and regulating my emotions. This can happen for several reasons, but one of the main ones for me is that I was taught the harder feelings are not OK or safe to feel. This can lead to having anger issues, as it did with me. I had a very volatile personality; there was no in between with me. It was 0 to 100 in seconds. I'd end up locking myself away in a bedroom for hours upon hours, isolating myself and my emotions in my safety cell. I questioned whether I should cry or not, whether to let my feelings out or keep them locked away, which I did for many years. Children may witness and experience things that will affect their adulthood and deliver them a journey they never chose to be on.

One way to heal my trauma was to convince myself I wasn't a broken soul and that many of the situations I'd experienced weren't my fault. My mind and my body wanted resolution. I had to heal my trauma and replenish my nervous system. For me to progress, I had to remove the negative people from my life, and that included family members who drained my energy, specifically one person who made my life a pure misery. I was afraid if I didn't deal with my childhood trauma, the rest of my life was going to be taken over by depression and ill health. I was continuously overthinking, which was exhausting. You cannot heal if you are continuously overthinking. When you are struggling and ready to throw in the towel, take a moment to think about the power of hope, the belief that something better is always possible if you are willing to work for it. If you work hard enough for it and believe in yourself, trust me, you can be whatever you want to be in life. Don't wait for motivation to come along and say hello: it's not just going to turn up on your doorstep. You have to make it happen. You need to take action to create the process. Nothing is impossible, regardless of the limitations others may place on us.

Healing from my trauma was like a butterfly learning to spread its wings for the first time. I wasn't losing my identity; I was regaining it. I had healed beyond all recognition. It was now time to step forward into a new chapter of my life.

✳✳✳

For the healing process to work, you need to look deeply into yourself. I will show you some key areas that might prevent you from healing.

Overthinking depletes your energy, and because everything is energy, everything needs to work in harmony for the healing process to happen. Well-being is paramount for a happy life. We have one chance to live on this earth – why waste it living in the past when tomorrow may be beautiful? Rather than think about things you are afraid of or worried about, why not start to think about the things you love, the things you are passionate about. Use that passion to fuel your well-being and to paint an image in your mind of what you want in life. The brain responds to repetition, imagery and emotion. Once you learn to become aware of your thoughts, you can let go of any negative ones and start to create new, positive ones.

Your subconscious mind is your superconscious mind. Don't call it subconscious: it knows more than you give it credit for. You have limited awareness, but your superconscious mind knows absolutely everything. Here's what you do. Ask yourself: who am I, what do I want, what is my purpose, what do I want to contribute, what kinds of friendships do I want to have, what unique skills and talents do I have? These questions will deliver solutions in the form of ideas or meeting people on your wavelength. Do a file search on yourself and it will deliver the answers directly to you when you need them.

In order to heal completely you need to stop quitting on the idea of positivity. If you keep quitting, you never really bought into the idea of stepping forward in life. The very second you think of something, it is stored in your mind. When you become emotionally involved, you're connected on a spiritual or emotional level, which then expresses itself through the body. The body is just an instrument of your mind. Your mind can make or break your body.

Spiritual healing involves the transfer of energy from the healer to the recipient, to release tension and strengthen the immune system. Spiritual healing is natural and non-invasive and has the intention of bringing the recipient into a state of balance. Spiritual healing is not faith healing – even the most sceptical of people can be healed – it's the transfer of energy from one person to another. I strongly believe in spiritual healing for many reasons. I believe firmly in a higher power. The word spiritual originates from the Latin word *spiritus*, meaning breath of life. The spiritual aspect of spiritual healing refers to energy working at a deep level on our spiritual being. The healer transfers the energy; in other words, the healer links with universal or divine energy to channel the healing for the mind, body and spirit. Universal or spiritual (non-religious) energy can be directed by intention. Aura (human energy) can raise spiritual vibration, improve health and allows one's highest nature to unfold.

Going back to anxiety, fear and anger, how many people carry these emotions around, like an energetic burden? Spiritual healing can release negative energy, speed up recovery and promote good health. It can help people with long-term mental and physical health conditions such as depression, stress, anxiety, bipolar disorder, backache, arthritis and cancer more comfortable.

✳✳✳

One laboratory experiment proved the mechanism of healing from one person to another via channelling energy. Electromagnetic experiments have shown that frequency magnetic fields were measured from the hands of the healers, not from their internal current alone. Electroencephalograms have demonstrated increased alpha brain waves in the healer and how a patient's brain waves change to synchronise with the healer's. Indeed, studies have shown it is possible to heal from a distance. Distant intention experiments using functional magnetic resonance imaging (MRI) seem to support the notion of distant healing. The possibility of two minds connecting with no verbal contact has been proved many times. Thus, there seems to be evidence of an energetic connection between individuals. This then indicates people can make other people's frequency higher.

✳✳✳

You have to trust and have faith in whatever process you use for healing your mind, body and soul. When I wish to channel positive energy, I look into the person's eyes, as if I'm looking into their soul. If they have a black cloud in their eyes, I send them a good vibe – maybe a smile, a simple hello, a compliment, even a hug. When I do, I witness a black cloud of negative energy leave their body. I then take note of how they react – and I guarantee you they smile. It's a very simple process of delivering positive energy and, even if only for a few seconds, lifting someone's vibrational frequency to a better place than it was before. A smile or a hug can help us recover faster from stress and even reduce our heart rate. It's magical and it costs nothing to be nice and share your well-being with other people.

I strongly don't recommend taking medication to feel better. I would rather use the natural route than medication. I don't want to fill my body with chemicals, only to cover up the real problem underneath. However, I am no doctor, and finding a beautiful, natural way of healing instead worked for me. I have gone from being suicidal to writing my second book, something I never thought possible. I intend to write children's books, too, to bring awareness to healing and well-being from an early age. Maybe we can all learn to love unconditionally and smile for one another.

Happy people seem to enjoy better health and longevity. Let's make happiness contagious. Happiness and glowing well-being can light up a room. What a beautiful sentiment indeed.

"Every step taken in mindfulness brings us one step closer to healing ourselves and one step closer to healing our planet."

— *THICH NHAT HANH*

Chapter 10

The Universe is Talking to You

This chapter opens the doors to the universe and its voice. The universe has different ways of sending us signs and guidance. If you learn how to recognise them, you could also learn to have a happier life. We're not talking about a voice you can physically hear – this is a lot simpler and less strange. The cosmos we live in is alive and we are connected to it in the grand web of life. It communicates with us naturally, through situations, people and signs. This isn't the first sign of madness, trust me; it's the first sign of an awakening.

Have you ever sat and had a random idea pop into your head, totally out of the blue, and wondered to yourself where on earth it came from? Well, it didn't come from the earth – it came from the universe. One of the top signs the universe is talking to you is a single dominant thought suddenly jolting you. This might come with an answer, a warning, an inspiration, or even advice. This random thought won't be something ordinary, like how much you enjoyed a fried breakfast, it's likely to be along the lines of realising a possible solution to a situation that's been plaguing you, or an overwhelming certainty of what you should say regarding a possible job offer, a warning about an upcoming event, or something about a loved one or family member whom you feel are in trouble of some kind. Thoughts like these indicate the universe is talking to you.

At times the universe likes to play little jokes and make fun with us. Sometimes it gives physical signs. You may be wanting to invest in a project, but you're being told conflicting advice. Some people are advising you go for it; others are telling you not to believe in the hype around it. You might pass a shop with a poster in the window that says *Seat belts save lives. It's not just law, it's common sense.* What that message is trying to tell you is, use your common sense and keep safe when it comes to investing. This is just one example of how a message may come to you from the universe.

What about gut feeling? Have you ever had that niggling feeling not to "go there"? Or there's something about someone you just don't connect with? This is the universe's energy trying to connect with your energy to tune into your frequency and talk to you. The only way it knows how is by sending messages for you to take notice of. These messages are there for absolutely everybody – it's down to the individual to seek and acknowledge them.

The modern world is fast-paced, and this pace leaves us with real problems. One such problem is social media. Observing and comparing other people's lives, staring at a screen all day at work, sitting on the train looking at your mobile phone, then going home to watch TV, if not your phone again. Technology is draining for the mind and makes us lose touch of reality and what signals to listen to.

The reactions of your physical being are more than just random chemical reactions; there is the wisdom of the cosmos filtering into you and sending your brain signs about what to do. Aches, pains, energy, exhaustion, restlessness, deep calm – these are all examples of how the universe is talking to you through your body.

You can receive messages from other people too. You're connected to the universe and the wisdom of life, and so is everyone around you. One of the top ways to know the universe is talking to you is to listen hard to those around you. This will often bring you what you need to know and when you need to know it, like an email that arrives just in time or a text message that pops up suddenly that changes your week, month, or even your year. The universe will speak to you through other people, calling you out of your shell and out of your confusion into a role and a mission that has been created for you. The universe wants to let you know about your spiritual calling. It is all a matter of discernment and learning to filter the proactive messages from the white noise.

After losing Lyrah, I shut out the world. I didn't even want to listen to the radio or watch television. One day, a song entered my mind, one that truly blessed me. That song was 'Somewhere Over the Rainbow'. As I went through every word of that song, I had a warm feeling of comfort and a memory of when I organised little Lyrah to be taken to Hamleys toy store in London, in a stretch limo full of balloons and toys. That memory opened my spirit. 'Where troubles melt like lemon drops, away above the chimney tops, that's where you'll find me. Somewhere over the rainbow, way up high.' That's an honest indication of how the universe sends us messages from another level of life. I strongly believe we live on after this physical life, as energy. A beautiful force was letting me know Lyrah was safe. I don't believe death is the end; I sincerely believe that. This is an example of how a song came into my mind, into my soul, and linked me with Lyrah. God's Kingdom is energy. Sometimes the universe doesn't talk to you; it sings to you.

***

Life will throw us many obstacles. Nothing is ever easy. Plans and dreams go wrong all the time; we all have setbacks. That's life. You can dust yourself off and try a new approach, reassess your goals or try again until you succeed. But one of the strongest signs the universe is talking to you is when setbacks and strange misfortunes hit you on a goal or project that should have been straightforward. You're just doing your thing and everything you attempt goes wrong, and you ask yourself why. Sometimes the universe is sending you an express mail with a simple message: this path, this job, this person, this place is not for you. It's that gut feeling again.

I know many of the things I didn't expect to work out actually turned out to be incredible opportunities and amazing guiding lights, especially later in life. And some opportunities which I expected to work failed. Some things are just not meant to be. I wrote my first book during my counselling with Julie, and writing it shone a new energy into my soul. It became my life force. This showed me the power of the universe is the unity of all, and it is within us all. If you tap into this amazing energy, you will find its power.

✴✴✴

This next one is a strange example, but I will share it with you anyway. Sometimes, one of the best ways to know the universe is talking to you is when you trip over what it is you need to know. Stumbling on lost items or household objects can be the wake-up call you've been needing to snap out of a trance or a low period. Maybe when rifling through your computer one evening you come across the profile of an old schoolfriend you haven't thought of in years. So, with that, you decide to contact them and then you discover they live near you. That's an example of the universe talking to you. Search and discover: the signals and messages are there.

I love the universe and how it works. It will show you different ways, signs and signals. It will show you its connection with you. Another sign the universe is talking to you, which is sort of the opposite of hitting unexpected snags and problems, is when there's a happy coincidence, unexpected help, amazing luck, and success on a project or decision that comes out of the blue. When you commit boldly to the true mission and desires of your soul, everything starts to move in your favour; the wheels start rolling towards a brighter horizon.

✴✴✴

I want to talk more about that gut feeling you have when something isn't right. Your gut is obviously a physical location in your stomach, but it's also an emotional centre. In many forms of meditation, breathing from the gut via techniques such as oceanic breathing bridges the gap between your conscious and unconscious while you enter a state of deep communication with the universe. Your gut is a powerful indicator of perception. Not only is good gut health integral to your mental and emotional health, your gut instinct is also a barometer for truth and safety. Gut feeling isn't the same as impulse. Your gut instinct has far more to do with what is right and logical. It tells us to embrace or step away, whether it's about staying in a job or a relationship, or leaving it. Gut instinct tells you something isn't right. Trust in your gut and use it as your guide. This is the universe connecting with your vibrational frequency, your energy. It's trying to keep you safe.

Sometimes, the universe gives us a little nudge at the right time. Say you're considering moving to a new area, but you have a lot of unanswered questions: will it work? Is it going to ruin my finances? Will I miss my neighbours and the friends I've made? Then a message comes out of the blue. You find out a friend lives there; you start chatting with a local business owner, who tells you they grew up in the place you're thinking about moving to and how much they miss it. Pay close attention, especially if these things happen more than once or right around the time when you need to make your decision.

✳✳✳

I wish to touch on some things that could be a sign the universe is talking to you. In my experience, numbers are one such sign. They're ways of spurring you into, or reminding you to take, action. You might see your school football shirt number popping up in random places, as a reminder to get in touch with your friends from school. Or you might keep seeing the date of your mother's birthday, as a nudge to pay more attention to her. I kept on seeing 777. When I researched it, I found out 777 is an angel number and it was indicating to me to take time to focus on myself and figure out where I'm heading. 777 encourages connection to the light, to manifest a bright future.

When the same thing keeps happening for no apparent reason, it could be the universe trying to get through to you. To be able to tell the difference, you need to think about whether it's the kind of thing that's unusual to repeat. If it's getting a call from your friend every Friday night or having cravings for burgers at lunchtime, there's nothing unusual about that and it's likely nothing to do with the universe. If you've been watching gardening videos on YouTube, it's hardly surprising your Facebook feed keeps giving you ads for a local nursery. That's not the universe trying to talk to you: that's advertising ads linked to your web search.

For universal signs, look for things like hearing about a new philosophy or idea from completely unconnected places, right when you've been looking for answers. Hearing a song over and over in different locations that you haven't heard in years has a strong message. As does randomly meeting someone in multiple places who you haven't seen for a long time. Analysing these patterns on your own can be overwhelming, but they are all signs from the universe.

Sometimes the universe leads you by your nose. I would definitely say a sense of smell can alert us to danger, excite us sensually, disgust us, intoxicate us and make us curious. Certain smells will give you a good or a bad memory of your childhood. Then there's our pheromones: invisible smells that help attract or repel those around us. Smell matters. And sometimes smell can be the universe talking to you about what to do, where to go or what to focus on. Never underestimate the ability of the universe to lead you to your destiny by your nose.

Animals also signify connection with the universe. Since ancient times animals have been an important part of spiritual guidance and meaning. The Ancient Egyptians had animal gods and many other cultures attribute animals to spiritual and metaphysical abilities, including Aztec, Mayan, Native American, Ancient Chinese, Arabic and certain African tribes. Animals can be spirit guides and symbols, providing comfort during dark times.

I'll give you a prime modern-day example. I've mentioned my beautiful cat, Poppy. Poppy feels and knows my every emotion. When I lost my mother, the energy within the home was strong, in a way that you could feel the atmosphere was dark and tense. When I'd get home, I'd return to an energy void – that missing energy being my mother. But when I walked through the door, Poppy would run and greet me with her squeak. In my darkest days, she would lie beside me and not leave my side. She vibed my energy. We have a very spiritual connection, and she always brings me a smile.

Animals connect with you spiritually, whether you're sad or happy. They are a powerful indication of mutual vibrational energy and frequency. When little Lyrah was battling her last hours of life, her ginger cat curled up on her chest and stayed with her till she passed away. Just watch the way a cat moves, or the affection a dog gives its owner. Take note of their actions and you will see what I mean. It's as if they're talking to you.

✳✳✳

What about the power of the spoken and written word? Words are powerful. In Christianity, the concept of *logos*, or the divine word, is at the foundation of the gospel. The book of John starts by saying: *In the beginning was the Word, and the Word was with God, and the Word was God.* The universe uses spoken and written words to communicate with you in ways that resound and carry forward into your life and future. It could be advice from a friend or loved one, or even a passage from a holy book or philosophy article. Graffiti on the side of a railway bridge may give you a sign. There will be something about that message that will stick with you and penetrate your soul, and it may apply directly to a major challenge, question or decision in your life. That's the universe using the power of words to talk to you.

✳✳✳

Dreams are another indication the universe is trying to contact you. The cosmos sneaks past our hypercritical conscious mind and enters our subconscious mind. It imparts wisdom, warnings, hope and heartfelt truth. In between the tossing and turning you may have while you're dreaming, you may have guides placing you in directions you might not have expected. And when you wake, you link with your gut instinct, which I talked about earlier. I have had some wonderful dreams, where I believe another world was trying to contact me. Just days after losing my mother, I was lying on the bed with a broken heart, wanting to smell and feel her close to me. I remember slowly drifting off to sleep, and an ice-cold breeze brushing past my face, which almost took my breath away. It was cold but comforting. I remember reaching out to embrace the wind, yet my arms were down beside me. It was my spirit reaching out to my mother's spirit. Energy upon energy. This happened on two occasions during the first few seconds of my dream state. This was my mother comforting me and letting me know she was OK. Dreams play a huge part in connecting with the universe.

Getting invited to something unexpected is another way of the universe trying to talk to you. Sometimes the universe presents you with an invitation or opportunity which jogs something in the back of your mind. This strange feeling – gut instinct – is telling you maybe you should go to that event. Maybe it would be fun and beneficial. So, you go, and it takes you down a whole new path, leading you to the life of your dreams. You hear stories of people going to parties they didn't want to go to but end up meeting the loves of their lives there. Life works in truly funny ways, and so does the universe.

Unexpected coincidences – I have had so many unexpected coincidences throughout my life. One after another. At times, they will give you a clue. This could be meeting someone who you're meant to be with. It could be finding a new job, just when you've come to the realisation your current position is no longer working for you. If the universe wants your attention, the least you can do is give it back. I truly believe that when the universe is talking to you, it's doing it for a reason: to guide you, help you, inspire you, warn you, rejuvenate you. You learn to recognise when the universe is talking to you, and, trust me, the conversation between you and the cosmos is definitely one worth having.

Then there are sudden waves of emotion. Just like before, when I talked about those sudden unexpected thoughts which break through the gloomy routine and show you the way, sudden waves of emotion can overpower you yet show you the way. Next question is, how do you separate hormones, random mood swings and real signs from the universe? The best way, in my view, is to look at the duration and the intensity of the emotion. Does it come and go like a summer storm and you never think of it again? Or is it lasting, deep and real? If it's the latter, then you're likely on the line with the universe.

✳✳✳

The positivity that can be gained from listening to the universe is beyond words. Observing signs from the universe is just one way to understand you're ready to see things from a new perspective. It's important to note we are the creators of our lives and we work with the universe as co-creators. The universe is there to help us and to give us pointers when we get lost. When we start veering in the wrong direction, we have to listen to the signs. Observing signs allows us to take the pressure off ourselves for making everything happen. Knowing we have guidance really relieves that pressure. Just remember we still have a responsibility to make things happen for ourselves.

Have you ever said to yourself, I need some help, please give me a sign? I have, many times. A sign could be a symbol, thing, person, number. When you declare you need a sign from the universe, ask it to show you something specific. You're then opening up a direct line of communication and showing you're ready to listen.

✳✳✳

The universe is sending you messages every single day. At times you may find your ego and unconsciousness are always looking for a way to explain them away. I have had moments while standing at my mother's and father's graves, deep in thought of the happy memories we shared, when all of a sudden, the wind's picked up. I take that as a message. It's so easy to have default behaviour, but I embrace every message that comes my way. Whether you believe in these messages is for you to decide. If something makes you smile and makes others smile in the process, then what a delivery of energy that is. If something around you lifts your mood, that is a message. Have an open mind. Take note of these emotions and everything the universe is showing you. Trust in these words and your life will change for the better. Nobody can be separated from the spirit – we are the spirit. Your being is within God, the God of energy.

✳✳✳

If you haven't already experienced an awakening, if you have not connected with the universe before, then know this: your awakening starts right now. You reading this book is a message from the universe to guide your spirit on a more positive journey. The universe saved my life. I was rushed into the resuscitation unit with a drink and drug overdose and suspected heart attack from attempting suicide, but I'm still here. Something guided me safely back to life. I believe in the spirit world and that our bodies live on as energy after physical life. I am still here for a reason, for a purpose. I absolutely believe that.

Every person and every experience that enters your life is a lesson in some way. You are attracted to your current state of consciousness and so if you want to attract different opportunities, you need to be willing to initiate a change of frequency and thought. When you start asking the universe for guidance, it raises your energy and your level of consciousness. You'll be more aware of your environment, and your energy will begin to attract a new set of experiences. Because we are co-creators of our destinies, we also have the power to create and manifest events. You can send your requests to the universe and have it echo them. If you're looking for a new relationship, a new job, a way to earn money, or simply a peaceful solution to a situation, develop a relationship with the universe. If you are new to the law of attraction and the workings of the universe, it may be useful to start developing a relationship with the universe so you can see for yourself how it works.

What you need to do is cultivate the desire for what it is you wish to receive. This is a valuable yet often overlooked starting point for any kind of life explanation. Pay attention. The universe doesn't have limits on how it speaks with you. Fine-tune your sensitivity and let it work its magic in its own special way. Remember this: the universe, the divine energy, won't give you what you want. The law of attraction will reflect what you are and the law of resonance will become what you manifest.

To complete this chapter, I'd like to touch on when your gut feeling lets you down, even though you believe it to be right. You may then ask yourself why the universe has not delivered. My answer to this is that we can't access all the information we need to guarantee ourselves success. We are often guided by gut feeling or intuition, which is defined as the immediate understanding, knowledge or awareness derived from neither perception nor reasoning. Research has shown me that feeding intuition with subliminal emotional information can improve the speed and accuracy of conscious emotions and decisions. The only way I can describe this is that if something is meant to be, it will be. The universe will guide you regardless of your intuition or gut feeling. It will lead you, in its own way, to find other messages linking you to your right path.

This chapter will hopefully guide you in the right direction to being aware of your connection with the universe.

"Everything in the universe is within you. Ask all from yourself."

— *RUMI*

Chapter 11

Pure Unconditional Love

Unconditional love and compassion are the highest vibrations of love and are not subject to preconditions, limitations, or requirements of others. They serve the greater interest and benefit of all sentient beings and their environment. Unconditional love, simply put, is love with no strings attached. It's love you offer freely. You don't base it on what someone does for you in return; you simply love them and want nothing more than their happiness.

Throughout my younger years, I never understood this beautiful quality, to love unconditionally. Human nature in my opinion has lost a very valuable quality, and that is to love purely. I was certainly one of those people. In my previous relationships, I placed conditions to my love, which is morally wrong. To a degree, we're all guilty of this offence – and it is an offence, because love with conditions is not true love.

I never really understood love either. I knew how to show it, but I never knew how to receive it. When I was seven, I was sexually abused, instigated by a family member, whom I trusted, admired and loved. My innocence in not realising the severity of their actions led me onto an unsure journey. Unbeknown to me at this point, this destroyed love in my heart and, over a period of years, the emotional abuse from the very same person destroyed my understanding of it. My mother and my father were not of the loving kind. It was not their fault: children of their era were brought up very differently. I would have loved a warm hug or heard those magic words "I love you". But those words were never spoken to me at all.

When I say those words now, I feel magical energy in the centre of my chest. That purity resonates with truth. "I love you" – aren't those words so beautiful, so meaningful? Feel their beauty, feel their meaning, welcome their energy as it is powerful beyond all words. Let those words embrace your heart, your centre point of your chest. There are no conditions; there are no strings. Live to love with a heart that makes people feel truly loved.

Material things mean absolutely nothing to me. Yet, give me your true love either in a relationship or as a friend and you will feel a love from me that will lift your vibrational frequency. That is what I wish for in my life – and that true unconditional love.

To heal myself and understand love on a pure level, I started to research the meaning of real love. I looked at why relationships very rarely last these days. The older generation seem to have it worked out – with couples together for decades, in some cases fifty years – so why aren't relationships working in the same manner in today's society? Is it the pressure of the world we live in? Have people changed to the point of living without love because it has become too complicated?

But let's be careful: just because unconditional love is beautiful, it doesn't mean it's weak. I love the thought that someone or something could love you without any conditions to their love. People sometimes link 'beautiful' with 'fragile'. The radiant vibrational energy omitted by that magic word 'unconditional' resonates love so delicately yet more powerfully than anything in the universe. Why? Because it's not selfish; it's self-transcendent.

When you feel unconditional love, you don't think, "If I could just be motivated by unconditional love all the time, everything would work out the way I want it to." It's more like, "When I'm motivated by unconditional love, I accept my actions, and my failures, and that I am a small part of a larger whole." And to pre-empt another common misconception, accepting outcomes doesn't mean enjoying or agreeing with them. A mother motivated by unconditional love who finds her child horribly injured doesn't enjoy that outcome or agree it's the right outcome. She feels grief and pain and anger, and eventually acceptance, then gratitude. That's the power and the essence of unconditional love: deep acceptance and gratitude for what is true. You might think deep acceptance would lead to complacency. If I accept every outcome, why should I do anything for myself or anyone else? You might just have to take my word for it, but regardless of what should happen logically, sitting around and doing nothing is not what happens when you experience unconditional love for yourself or for others.

Unconditional love and the accompanying acceptance of what is true leads to major positive transformation. I hope you understand what I'm trying to convey here. It may not make sense yet, but give it time. There's some kind of causal loop ingrained in our souls. It's like unconditional love is what makes practical time travel possible, and practical time travel helps create unconditional love.

Everyone seems to have their own definitions of what love is. Some people think of love as an act of extending their hands to those who need help; some people think love is about giving people opportunities to help themselves so they can grow stronger. Some people see love as working overtime without pay. Some people think jealousy is a form of love. So, what is love? I have explained how I feel love should be expressed. Universal love is a state of mind, and like all states of mind, it can be refined to higher degrees. Like a piece of coal that can be refined to a diamond, love can be refined from being a conditional action to the higher state of unconditional love.

We can look to nature for examples because it's there where unconditional love is in abundance. Trees, for instance, love everything unconditionally. Trees don't run away from an incoming storm, but accept it with open arms. What about water? You can observe the movement of love as you pour hot water into a cup of cold water and the two strive to reach a balance with each other. What about the way the sun gives out its life unconditionally for our benefit? You can see love in the way nature has always been honest with itself. Fire will always be fire. Water will always be water. Every element in nature will stay true to itself, unlike humans, who can distort the truth and lie through appearance.

The more you look for examples of unconditional love in the universe, the more you will find. Realise that, at the end of the day, the quest for the true definition of love is not to simply arrive at it, rather to refine it. Thus, to know what love is, is to know more about what you already know. Otherwise, your knowledge of it can't remain subjective and unrefined. So, let the universe and your life experiences teach you about what love is every day so that you can know even more about it.

As I have explained to you, lacking love as a child affected me as an adult. I had to address the darkness in my mind. I had to experience a brighter life. The more you develop knowledge of what love is, the more you will be able to transform unhappiness into happiness. Why is this? Because the only way to transform mental suffering – fear, anger, impatience – is to develop greater love for yourself and others. The more we can learn about love, the more we will progress on that journey.

Perhaps we can learn more about love through understanding that it's a state of mind rather than an action. Learn the importance of balancing love with wisdom. To love everything is to love oneself, and to love oneself is to love everything. There is no greater happiness than to know and love oneself. We have to learn to love who we are before we can learn more about the meaning of love. The journey of self-transformation really is a journey of refining your knowledge of love.

Prior to my awakening, I had no understanding of what love should feel like. I had to learn to refine myself and accept myself and my past to be able to reflect on tomorrow. Until you accept all your demons, you won't be able to step forward into the light and find the meaning of love. You need to work on your state of mind, because your state of mind will determine your ability to learn about true love. How can you forgive when you're angry? How can you love fearlessly when you're afraid? How can you love patiently when you don't have patience?

Instead of focusing your energy on analysing what love is, you need to learn what actions are loving and what actions are not. By working on your mind, you will naturally come to realise what love is. Once the darkness is illuminated, you will find the state of unconditional love you've been searching for has always been there, right inside you. That is because love has always been your most natural state of being, for you are made of love in the same way as the universe is. The spiritual journey of developing the knowing of love is therefore a journey of self-remembering.

The universe is based on unconditional love. We live in a harmonious universe that is founded upon a conscious and loving energy. The conscious field is constantly vibrating and flowing, changing and creating our world. It can be found in all things, in all atomic structures, finding and connecting. The principle of resonance connects everything: what we give out is what we receive. If we choose to love each other, that's what we get back. Love can change the vibrations in the field to harmony.

The essence of love is to affirm as well as unselfishly delight in the well-being of others, and to engage in acts of care and service. Unlimited love extends to all others without exception, in an enduring and constant way. Widely considered the highest form of virtue, unlimited love is often deemed a creative presence that is integral to reality: participation in unlimited love constitutes the full experience of spirituality.

For me to move on in my life I had to forgive people from my past for stealing my love. Forgiveness is part of unconditional love and is extremely important to well-being. Forgiveness studies suggest that a person who forgives is happier and healthier. Benefits of forgiveness include decreased levels of anger and hostility, increased feeling of love, increased ability to trust, liberation from traumatic experiences, no more repetitive negative behaviour patterns, increased physical health and remarkable recovery from psychiatric dysfunctions. On the other hand, if you are unable to forgive, you might suffer on a mental, physical and emotional level.

Up until I began counselling, I was living a complete lie. The person I had become was not the real me. Unless I dealt with my trauma, I was never going to move to a positive life filled with love. Reliving my trauma and forgiving the person who did me harm had a dramatic effect on my health, but, as I discovered, forgiveness frees mental and emotional energy, which improves performance even in completely unrelated tasks. The biggest challenge is to forgive yourself. I had hurt a lot of people and put my emotional stress onto them, including my parents. Forgiving is easier when we remember that everything that happens in our lives has a higher meaning. We are here to experience challenges to learn from them, and those who bring us challenges are our teachers.

The most shocking thing is many of us don't love ourselves unconditionally. Before I could step forward into the new chapter of my life, I had to learn to love myself unconditionally. How many times have you heard people say they love and accept themselves as they are? We have inferiority complexes because we don't love ourselves. We say negative things about ourselves because we don't love and accept who we are.

***

I stumbled across an energy named by scientists as 'Zero Point Field'. This truly intrigued me as it indicates the pattern of the flower of life, the tapestry upon which our entire universe is painted. The strands of this tapestry, this energy, are forged from unconditional love. This means that the true binding force of the universe is love, and love is the way and the truth. The flower of life is the seed that holds our blueprint in our spiritual consciousness. We are a part of that field, and our consciousness can interact with it on many levels. At the core teaching of religious and belief systems is the fundamental nature of God's energy: love and light.

The flower of life symbol was known to the Ancient Egyptians. In Abydos, Egypt, three flower of life patterns can be seen in the pillars of the Osirion temple. The goddess Neith symbolises the cosmic process and was presented as a weaver of the world, a symbol of science and knowledge. The Ancient Egyptians knew that everything is created by thoughts. If you change the way you look at things, the things you look at change.

✳✳✳

Our minds and our intentions are very powerful. When we control our minds, we control our thoughts, and therefore our feelings, emotions and behaviour. We retain our power and don't let our desires, emotions, negative ego or inner child rule us. Mastering our minds creates an opportunity to always have peace of mind, to love unconditionally and to stay in a state of harmony and tranquillity, no matter what is going on around us.

If we observe our minds, we will find that we judge people before we love them. We judge actions, words, qualities and how we're treated and we reject anyone who doesn't fulfil these requirements. That isn't love; it's attachment. Attachment is a very biased system and it makes us selfish, because we constantly think in terms of "*I*". Do they treat "*me*" nicely? Do they take care of "*me*"? Can "*I*" relate to them? Do they match "*my*" social status? Anything that involves ego is most certainly not unconditional love. Unconditional love is loving people as they are and not trying to change them, no matter where they're from and how they look. Attachment is very complicated and superficial because it looks at appearance rather than soul.

Love is a personal journey and one that rules every aspect of life. I have learnt that unconditional love comes from the centre point of your heart. The heart remains open, non-judgemental and tolerant. We need to embrace this energetic energy. Generosity of spirit drives unconditional love, when the intentions of the heart are pure and without ulterior motive. Unconditional love can only exist when the intention is to create joy or ease suffering.

In my charitable work with sick and terminally ill children, when I give love, it's for their smiles. The motive behind my kindness is to see them smile in the darkest hours of their lives. If you are going to place a motive behind your kindness, make sure it's a sincere one. I like to express my love on a spiritual level, as pure energy. Expressing positive vibrations without any conditions is the only form of love I now understand.

Friendship is built on deep understanding. The intention in any friendship is to share joy and happiness, but if you don't understand what brings your friend joy, there can be no true love. When we fully understand our friends and without reservation, it is easy to love them. Compassion cannot exist if there is no desire to lessen or transform the suffering of our loved ones. Compassion can come in the form of a kind word, a loving gesture or a benevolent action, but the intent to lift another's suffering is a mark of true love. Bringing joy to people delivers communion. Love that does not bring mutual joy is not true love.

✳✳✳

As I mentioned earlier, non-attachment is the key element to unconditional love. Love placed in a vacuum would quickly die, but that is what happens to a loved one if the affection becomes possessive or clingy. This was my own downfall because I was starved of love as a child. I suffocated partners with text messages and constantly needing reassurance I was loved. I was incredibly clingy. My inner child needed to know he was truly loved. True love should never be a prison sentence.

Not everyone receives unconditional love from their parents. In my eyes, my mother was the most beautiful being a little boy could ever imagine. She was both angel and ally, the physical embodiment of a caring and undying love that permeated every aspect of my existence. The spiritual connection with my mother was so strong. When she passed away, part of my soul died with her. My inner child craved her love. A mother's love reaches way beyond the border of visible light.

When I visit my mother's and my father's graves, I place my hand firmly over their centre points, where their hearts are. I send a message from my centre point, and I tell them, "I love you." Not only do I receive energy from the graves themselves, I deliver energy to let them know how much I truly love them both. I now see life in a very different light.

✳✳✳

The world is your mirror and a reflection of your mind. If you believe the world is one of hatred and injustice, that is what you'll be greeted with every day. The hatred and injustice you rally against will become a self-fulfilling prophecy. Just as an enlightened person knows that lasting peace can never be attained through war, attempts to meet hatred with hatred will result in a stalemate, and no change will be able to occur. Only when you meet hatred with love and compassion does change have a chance. Then, you'll be modelling the behaviour you would like to see in others.

The cruel irony is that when you lower yourself to the level of your adversary or despised ideology, you become a vibrational match. Anger matched with anger only creates the same energetic vibrations. To change your reflection, change the way you view the world. If you have loving thoughts, the world will reflect your loving state of mind and you will see more love in the world. That won't end the hatred and injustice, but your decision to be loving means there's one less person in the world who hates. The exponential power of one person inspiring another (and then another) should never be underestimated. Since we already know that fighting anger with anger just creates more of the same, wouldn't love be a more positive behaviour to multiply?

Unconditional love is a natural restorative agent for the soul; a magical spiritual energy dispensed in generous amounts can turn around the perspective of even the most jaded soul. The power of unconditional love to heal is a gift of such life-changing proportions that if conveyed on a mass level, it could change the world. When love is not conditional, it's able to flow around the darkest, most painful areas of the soul, without judgement or intolerance. The effect can be instant. Even the most forgotten spirit annihilated by life, if able to make a significant change for the better, can undergo a dramatic awakening through the unconditional love of just one person.

Rejuvenated souls can heal multitudes because of the unconditional love of the single soul that started the chain reaction. The true power of unconditional love is profoundly impactful. Under the right conditions, unconditional love can be contagious; a viral agent that spreads its contagion in ways that could begin the evolution of a society.

Just remember the law of vibration and the law of attraction. The energy will guide you to the life you wish for and, in turn, deliver the sunshine of unconditional love in the magical way the universe does so beautifully.

"Unconditional love is our eternal universal bond to life itself."

— *HAROLD W. BECKER*

Chapter 12

Self-Discovery and Personal Vibration

There comes a point in life when a new chapter will arise. At this point, your consciousness hasn't begun to awaken from your true inner self, but it identifies what you have become and who you are possibly about to become. The beginning stages of self-discovery and personal vibration have begun to blossom.

What does an awakening feel like? What is this new identity? What does it mean? For me, that discovery started when I began to take more notice of the beautiful songbirds, the brightness of the sun, the glow of the moon and the beauty of the sky and the stars within it. I began to witness another side of life following a nervous breakdown and being diagnosed with PTSD. I was about to awaken into a beautiful resonance of energy.

I was drawn to spiritual teachings and nature. I began to take more notice of life around me – nature, the earth, the planets, the sky, the sun and the stars. When you awaken, you connect with your mind, subconsciously, consciously, spiritually. I strongly believe in the strength of the energy centre point, the heart. This amazing energy made me question who I am, what I had become and what I had achieved, and what I wish to achieve in the remainder of my life. My trigger points opened understanding. My life was about to change for the better, and for the better of those around me too.

If you have already had your awakening, you may relate to some of the content in this book. If you have not, then you are about to receive your awakening right here, right now. I want you to discover your identity. Let's pretend for a moment you have no past, no trauma, no issues from your childhood. In reality, there is no past, only the here and now. Let's also pretend there is no future – nothing to look forward to. Let's now strip away what you believe to be your identity – your past and your future. What is now left and what is now lost? Have a think about that. There is nothing you can now put an identity to. You have become your truest self since you don't remember your past. You're your truest self when there isn't a single thought in your mind. Take note of the stillness, without the identity you believed to be yours. The essence of your identity is now becoming clear. The light of pure consciousness is very much there. It's always been there, but it's more understandable and real now. You get a stronger sense of who you are when you don't tell yourself who you are. You are never truly more yourself than when you are still – when your mind is still.

Once you discover your identity, you are free of incompleteness, from who you believed was the real you. Dissatisfaction, fear, unease, trauma, the world, the past and the present – that wasn't the real you. The abused and bullied child lacking love from his parents was not my true identity. I wasn't complete and I wasn't happy. Releasing your true form to help others, love unconditionally and forgive others is the beginning of your truest self and the building blocks of an awakening. Before you can learn to manifest your future you need to build the foundation into that journey.

At the beginning of my awakening, I felt tired and drained. I couldn't work out why I couldn't recover from losing my mother and Lyrah. The thoughts, the dreams, the nightmares, my trauma, the lack of love from my mother, the battles I had looking after her, watching her choke to death on her own blood – all of this was contributing to my awakening. My past was not the real me – the violent person I'd become, the person who'd ended up in prison, the person manufactured from other people's doing.

I had to find an inner stillness and remove the negativity that energy had created, for it was dictating my future. As spiritual beings, we operate on vibrational frequencies. In order to connect to that divine frequency, we have to go through a conscious journey of spiritual awakening. There is another dimension that is not a physical world of consciousness, which delivers consciousness only experienced by the spiritually awakened. In other words, there is another entity of energy within that awakening. Ascension is the process of raising your vibration, shredding your ego and gaining control of your future through an elevated consciousness spaced on your birth chart, which is a calculation of your place of birth and time of birth.

My spiritual awakening took its toll on my body and affected my mental health, because in the process of spiritual awakening your senses are heightened to adjust to the new frequency. People operate on energy vibrations that are based on dimensions. You will experience several changes, physically and emotionally – don't be alarmed. Some people might go to the doctor's, complaining about feeling ill, or not quite feel themselves when there's actually really nothing wrong. When you realise there is more to life than you've previously perceived, it's at that point changes are happening. Have you ever analysed your life in detail, worrying about the things you should and shouldn't have done? The things you should have said? The achievements you could have achieved? And those failed relationships you never took the time to repair? If so, then you may be undergoing symptoms of ascension. You might feel anxious or confused. If you do, then don't be afraid: it's all part of the vibrational shift you will be going through into your awakening.

You will begin to stop judging yourself and other people. You will begin to experience the higher emotions and no longer tap into the lower ones. You came to earth to experience the lower emotions – that is what we are taught from a very early age – and this vibrates a negative like-for-like energy. You'll decide to no longer judge yourself or think of yourself as being different.

Don't for one minute think you are going mad. You are releasing the part of you that no longer serves you. You've evolved and are getting closer to your true self. You may feel a ringing in your ears or experience visions you don't understand. Just take a deep breath and let it go. Your mind is awakening.

The journey of spiritual awakening is a very personal experience, so it isn't easy to provide a single definition of what spiritual awakening means. But the common definition is that spiritual awakening is the intellectual, emotional and spiritual way in which an individual realises their true nature. It can lead to re-evaluations of your life and how you fit into the world around you. It may also be characterised by an increased sense of well-being or happiness. Many believe this change is triggered by a profound realignment in consciousness that makes sense of their past, present and future. The truth about spiritual awakening can't be learned from anyone other than yourself, because we all experience it differently. The next thing you'll want to figure out is what triggered your change. Before you can answer that, you'll need to look at your life.

No one can tell you why you are having this awakening, but it's worth a shot to ask anyone who may have an idea or experienced an awakening themselves. Some people prefer to scientifically frame their spiritual awakenings, by focusing on the physiological changes they experienced. Some people have changes to their metabolism, their blood pressure or their breathing patterns while they are going through an awakening. Some even claim to have seen the light or angels. It's not uncommon for people to feel confused; you might cry, laugh or be angry after an awakening. You go through a lot of bodily changes as well as changes to your mental well-being.

There are two things that most people experience after an awakening: a sense of newness and a sense of relief. Newness, because they feel happy, excited and curious; relief, because they feel at peace. People will tell you nothing in the world can compare to finally finding your place in the world.

Your body is just the carrier of your energy. I've said I believe that when we die, our energy lives on. Everything is energy. Our bodies are full of a vibrational frequency that does not die; it's eternal.

I have more compassion for others; less judgement. I have more clarity, more forgiveness, more love. I care more. A true awakening delivers gratitude. Be grateful for the person you are and live in hope that other people can forgive you for the person you once were. I am a spirit. I am a spiritual being within a physical body.

I believe we are all attached to a spiritual strength, like an umbilical energy. Once we learn to understand this, we can pursue our desires, our ambitions and, most of all, our truest form. Energy is everything. Please believe that.

Self-discovery can be quite frightening if you don't understand what it entails. What it delivers is self-awareness and reaching a point where you are ready to make the change. Essentially, you are becoming a new person – who you were originally supposed to be. It's unlearning everything you used as a coping strategy. You are going to notice things you were doing are no longer serving you; in fact, they never were in the first place.

As I have mentioned, I became the person I never chose to be, because I was programmed as a child. I had an older sister who bullied me, intimidated me and made me feel worthless for many years. So, if you are feeling overwhelmed or scared, I want to send this message of encouragement to you to let you know you are doing exactly what you need to be doing. You are exactly where you need to be, right here, right now. There's no rush. Don't push it to happen. Let it flow naturally. It's all part of the process. Being able to honour the point you are at is a blessing, and you will be able to look back at the first day you decided to figure out who you really are.

This journey of self-discovery and personal vibrational frequency takes courage. You will figure out who you want to be in life, so be kind to yourself. Ask yourself when was the last time you felt at peace. I had so many questions I needed to answer, but you too will wake up one day and everything will suddenly feel right. Your heart will be calm, your soul will be lit, your thoughts will be positive, your vision clear, and then it will happen. You will step into your life with a new sense of being. It's a beautiful element of wonder and excitement when you find yourself suddenly feeling very much alive.

Your spiritual awakening could well be spontaneous. My first signs were feeling disconnected and detached. I was overwhelmed and confused. It felt like everything I thought to be true about my life was a lie. Even my dreams are now more vivid than they've ever been. This is a true sign of an awakening. The desire to find meaning and fulfilment will become one of your biggest priorities. You'll have heightened intuition: you'll be able to sense inauthentic, deceptive or manipulative behaviour. You'll suddenly realise everyone else is on their own path while you're figuring out yours, and you'll be more accepting of it. Things like winning arguments or convincing people of your views won't matter as much because you'll understand every living thing is inherently worthy. You'll feel happy to be of service to people and the environment. It's important you have that calling to make your life feel purposeful. It may not be about changing your current role or job but approaching what you are already doing with a deeper sense of service. I am passionate about making dreams come true for sick and terminally ill children, and the elderly – whether that's a day at the seaside having fish and chips or simply someone to talk to. Your empathy will become more apparent.

Spiritual awakenings are no easy undertaking and while there's hope for enlightenment on the other side, it can feel very lonely. Having your whole life flipped upside down is isolating, especially if the people in your life aren't on your wavelength.

You may feel less connected to your friends and family and more connected to nature. You'll be tuned into the present moment, more sensitive to physical, emotional and energetic stimulation. Along with heightened awareness and senses, you may have physical sensations too. Sleep disturbances are not uncommon, nor are fatigue and brain fog. Some days, I wake feeling drained. When I do, I immediately give my affirmations for the day to lift my vibrational frequency to a stronger energy. As your spiritual life begins to transform, so will your day-to-day life, including your habits and routines. Perhaps now you'll make it a priority to spend time in nature or meditate or ditch old habits that are no longer serving you.

Spiritual awakening can result in alienation and ego-shattering realisations which can make you feel like you're living in a new reality. You'll be more empathetic, as you begin feeling more connected to the world around you. Other people's suffering may feel impossible to ignore. You're likely to feel more compassionate while still wanting to hold people accountable. And lastly, you will probably have a child-like wonder of the world around you, even when things get tough. Being able to stay curious about your life and the people in it, even when you're feeling emotional, is a sign of spiritual awakening.

To make space for a spiritual awakening, try and develop daily, weekly or monthly spiritual practices such as meditation, mindfulness and gratitude. Spiritual awakening is complicated, profound and nothing short of life-changing – but in the best way. While it may not be easy, with patience and trial and error, it will improve your life for the better. Trust the process, hang on tight and prepare for a newly awakened life.

"The privilege of a lifetime is to become who you really are."

— *CARL JUNG*

Epilogue

"I see skies of blue and clouds of white, the bright blessed day, the dark sacred night, and I think to myself what a wonderful world." Those beautiful, soul-warming words from the great Louis Armstrong. I share my research, my findings, my discovery and, of course, my 'awakening' of how truly magical and mysterious our beautiful solar system really is.

Science has taught us to rely on what we can feel and see. What we fail to engage with is our spiritual connections – our emotions, our thoughts and our bodies are all made up of vibrating energy. I confess to only my own personal awakening of this beautiful bright light of unconditional energy. I sincerely hope this book engages your energy to locate the path of love and light.

None of the content of this book is new knowledge, and I'm no scientist or expert. I was a soul that was lost and broken, and damaged beyond repair. Or so I thought. Here I am, writing my second book, sharing the new sentences of the new chapters of my life. I recovered and I completely turned my life around.

We all have a story to tell. It's the wisdom it delivers that we must embrace to become the person we want to be and the journey we want to be on. Ask yourself these questions. Do you know who you are? What is your purpose? Are you happy with your life? Are you content with just existing? Let me tell you something which will open your eyes. When your time comes to finally close your eyes on this life, will you look back over your time on this beautiful planet and feel content with your life? Will you wish you had taken chances? Did you live to your true potential? The forty years in a soul-destroying job that you hated waking up for each morning to go to work – was that wasted? You paid the bills, of course, but that was all you did. The moment your eyes close on that life is the moment you will have an awakening. But why not have that awakening now while you still have breath in your body? There are no excuses. So many people blame everything else on why they can't find their purpose in life. Oh, it's the kids, I can't. Oh, it's my job, I can't. Oh, it's too much for me to change.

I discovered why I am here. Finding such a powerful force of energy opened my third eye, my all-seeing eye, as to what this life is all about. I am so blessed to have received this information now rather than when I finally close my eyes on this life. Have your awakening now. Treat this as your message, as if the universe is talking to you too. Feel your personal vibration and work with the energy to transform your life. Don't let yourself be fooled and carried by external conflicting energies. You can create the path you wish to be on. You can learn to coach your mind and become aware of who you truly are, find your true frequency and create the life you wish. Learn how to raise your positive vibrations, your frequency, to benefit yourself as well as the environment around you. My awakening was the most valuable gift in my whole entire life. It saved me.

I have written this book with the intention to guide that one person who may need to find their light. When I overdosed on drink and drugs, my subconscious mind was in battle with my conscious mind. One part of me wanted to die; the other wanted to stay. How many people change their mind as they decide to take their own life? As my tongue twisted and my chest tightened, I knew my time was not done. I didn't want to die. Was that an awakening, you may ask? Yes, to a degree it was, as it was my first step to realising how precious life is. My spirit wasn't ready to depart this life for the next. The question is, is it possible to have subconscious suicidal thoughts that the mind is not aware of or is in conflict with? And if so, could someone act on them consciously? My past played a big part in attempting to take my own life. And witnessing my mother choking to death was the final nail in the coffin. I didn't care if I lived or died. I previously lacked the discipline to change my life; I failed to find the energy to lift my spirits to the point of return. Witnessing a nine-year-old little girl lose her life to an inoperable brain tumour, just days after my mother died, was a real test of strength. My past and present trauma combined beat my spirit into darkness.

I never knew or understood the value of life until I addressed my own, in that moment of my awakening. Daily meditation and affirmations build your vibrational energy. Affirmations sink into the subconscious mind and materialise the intention of your words into the outer world. This does not mean that every word will get results, but it trains your mind to trigger the subconscious mind into action. The words have to be said with attention, intention and feeling. I say my affirmations out loud, to send out my vibrational frequency and obtain positive results. We need to learn to use the conscious part of our minds more productively since everything else the brain doesn't do consciously but subconsciously, which can produce negativity. Do you tell your heart to beat? Do you remind yourself to blink? Do you tell your body when to release the right hormones? How about your memories? When a memory leaves your conscious mind, is it gone forever? Where does it go, and how can it come back? Everything is stored within the subconscious. Have you ever gone blank? You rack your brain, can't think of it and finally give up. And then, when you aren't even thinking about it, it suddenly pops into your head? You see, the subconscious never stopped looking for that memory. I like to think of the conscious mind as the main vibrational frequency for our complete operating system. It gives us control over what matters and leaves the rest to the automatic process. Our subconscious will apply that belief to everything automatically. It will protect that belief, it will confirm itself, it will make you notice things that confirm the belief and ignore what doesn't fit. This is what allowed me to download new beliefs and delete negative ones. Remember that we are unique beings and everything happens for a reason. Many of us never embrace our full potential. We all have a slice of God in us; we all have the ability to create miracles, save lives, create hope for one another. Find your inner wealth, make a difference to your time on this earth and resonate that vibrational energy to others for it to spread.

Use your conscious sensitivity physically and emotionally. Using conscious sensitivity gives you the ability to immediately perceive subtle stimulation from either physical or nonphysical sources and to discern what it means. I now have total clarity and a higher state of wisdom. I feel illuminated now my mind has awakened to its divine power. I now feel nothing can break me. I have taken life's beatings and am still standing. Lose your ego and find your purpose – ego separates you from reality. Find empathy in your soul as it will give you a greater understanding.

Use that gut feeling as I have written within this book. The chakra, the centre force located in the centre of your body, the spiritual force in the etheric body. That magical word 'intuition' the direct knowing of what is real in any situation without needing proof; the perception that occurs within the body, emotions, the mind and inner spirit are simultaneously active and integrated while being truly focused completely in the present moment; a state of perceptual alertness in which one feels intimately connected to all living things and experiences that are in tune with the nature of life. Remember the use of tuning your frequency into another. Tuning one's personal vibrations consciously or unconsciously to the vibration of another person for the purpose of communication. This will enable you to weed out people, situations and opportunities and align those vibrations that match and those that don't. Don't waste your time and energy on people that don't share your vibes. I wasted so many years on people who drained my energy, to the point where they'd drop me at the wayside when I was of no benefit to them. Get rid of all negativity, rid those negative people. For me this also went for certain members of my so-called family. Use your wisdom of past negativity and turn that energy around.

Find harmony in your life. Once you've gained wisdom in the transformation process, use that energy to improve your quality of life and for good things to come your way. Live to laugh and love unconditionally. You have one life, so if you have an ambition, then go get it, no excuses. Climb that mountain, run that marathon, run your own business, do what you love, and life will love you in return. Life will throw obstacles: it's what it does.

I never imagined I would become an author and here I am writing my second book, with more to follow. I love expressing my thoughts and emotions. My greatest therapy was writing *My Tormented Mind*.

I highly recommend writing your problems down, leaving them for a while and coming back to them. When you do, you will have a different point of view. I have found such beauty in life and as I write my final sentences, I know, on account of my awakening, there is more to life than just life itself.

I hope *The Awakening* will in some way be a gifted advisor. The universe loves you – unconditionally. Only you can put conditions on your love. The truth is, the nature of your thoughts are deeply intertwined with your physical reality (your health, career, success, relationships, etc.). The mental and the physical move in lockstep; they go hand in hand.

In basic terms, the law of attraction states that your thoughts and beliefs system sends certain vibrations out to the cosmos. In turn, the universe responds by giving you a kind of customised set of experiences which directly validate said thoughts and beliefs. If your mind is constantly negative, you will live a negative life and those around you will vibe your negativity – like attracts like. Do not self-impose limitations as these will prevent your dreams from becoming reality. Purify your intent. Personally, meditation puts the law of attraction squarely in my true energy. Meditation pulls the rug out from under low vibrational emotions such as anger, despair, shame, fear and regret and naturally clears the path for high-resonating emotions such as gratitude, joy, love and hope. I love the inner calm and stillness of mind meditation brings, shifting your vibration to a higher frequency, making you a permanent magnet for positive experiences. Make the change now and set your life on the best possible course.

Don't close your eyes on this life without having the courage to live a true life. Be true to yourself: don't live how others expect you to. Make that change now. Ninety per cent of people die with regret. There are a couple of reasons why. The first is other people holding us back. Another is people not knowing who they are and therefore not knowing what they want. Prior to my awakening, I felt my soul slowly dying. I could feel myself slipping into deep depression. This created habits I didn't need in my life, such as drinking and drugs. Stop doing what you know you're not supposed to be doing. Stop following what people say you should be doing. If you stay on the route you're on, if you don't love what you're doing, if you're not following your purpose in life, if you're not finding your dream, if you're not doing exactly what you want to do, then you'll end up part of the 90% of people who die with regret. Be brave, use your vision and purpose and don't live to the expectations and the opinions of others. Follow your dreams, achieve your own goals. Your journey is your journey: make it unique.

Your vibration controls your life, your progress, even your mental and physical health. Life is, most of all, about love. Smile and the rest of the world will smile with you. Look for the good in everyone you meet and rise above those who try to make you feel low. Fill your heart and your soul with unconditional love. Many people live their lives for 'someday'. They put their dreams on hold, waiting for the right time. Stop waiting for the right time – that day may never come. Your time is now. Don't just exist, live life to the fullest. It's time to stop letting the past define your future.

My awakening has given me a new lease of life. The new chapters of my new life are going to be bright and beautiful. I wish to say thank you from my spirit, heart and soul. May the great God of energy bless your journey ahead. Embrace the power of personal vibration and let the sun shine, the moon glow and the stars glitter brightly. May the universe align with you forever more.

I love you.

"With every sunrise, there is a new tomorrow. With every new tomorrow, there is a new beginning."

— *ROCKY TROIANI*

To the Reader

If this has happened to you, then you will understand everything I'm about to say. At some point in your life, you will experience a spiritual awakening. It might be triggered by an extreme event or a crisis, maybe by a chronic illness, or it might simply be the natural process of your soul maturing.

At the beginning of an awakening, we begin to ask big questions. What is my purpose? What is the meaning of life? What happens after we die? An awakening is often triggered by the feeling that something profound is missing in our lives. A good number of people sadly don't have faith or belief in themselves. They continue to take the blue pill and remain in comfortable ignorance because taking the red pill would mean everything they ever knew was false, and facing that pain would be too scary.

You on the other hand will hit that moment in your life where you suddenly realise you don't have to do the same thing over and over – you have a choice. There are two kinds of people on this earth: the ones who need to be told and the ones who figure it out for themselves. You'll begin to think about things you told yourself long ago that you shouldn't have. But once you let down those walls of fear, you'll begin to see things for what they really are. Most of you will remember when this happens to you. You will become highly sensitive to the suffering of others and feel cut off from the world – cut off from the divine almost – and the more aware you become of your disconnection, the more it will hurt you. You will have this ache deep inside that never seems to stop, but know that before we see the light, we have to walk through the dark, cold valley of the shadow of death to prepare our hearts and our minds for what we are about to receive. Think about it this way: in order to put on new clothes, the old ones have to make way for the new. You'll start to perceive reality in a totally different way. You'll see through the lies and the delusions. You'll feel unhappy with how things are, and you'll be disturbed by the suffering you see. You'll no longer see life how you once did; you'll start seeking truth in everything you do and you won't be afraid of the answers because you're craving the light. You'll soon realise you're not alone in this quest and you are one of hundreds and thousands all becoming awakened to the truth, pretty much at the same time. Embrace it. Visualise the most beautiful, brightest light you've ever seen, welcoming you as you walk towards it. Feel the calm of its beauty and the truth of its unconditional love, which will live in your soul for eternity.

L'alam al-mein. Aa-meen: "I seal this prayer in trust and faith and truth."

The Lord's Prayer in Ancient Aramaic.

Milton Keynes UK
Ingram Content Group UK Ltd.
UKHW020250081223
434001UK00004B/40